D1575622

RADICALIZING HER

RADICALIZING HER

WHY WOMEN CHOOSE VIOLENCE

NIMMI GOWRINATHAN

BEACON PRESS
BOSTON

BEACON PRESS
Boston, Massachusetts
www.beacon.org

Beacon Press books
are published under the auspices of
the Unitarian Universalist Association of Congregations.

24 23 22 21   8 7 6 5 4 3 2 1

This book is printed on acid-free paper that meets the uncoated paper
ANSI/NISO specifications for permanence as revised in 1992.

Text design and composition by Kim Arney

Some names and identifying details in this book have been
changed to protect the privacy of individuals.

Library of Congress Cataloging-in-Publication Data

Names: Gowrinathan, Nimmi, author.
Title: Radicalizing her : why women choose violence / Nimmi Gowrinathan.
Description: Boston : Beacon Press, [2021] | Includes bibliographical
    references and index.
Identifiers: LCCN 2020048138 (print) | LCCN 2020048139 (ebook) |
    ISBN 9780807013557 (hardcover) | ISBN 9780807013601 (ebook)
Subjects: LCSH: Women radicals—Case studies. | Women soldiers—Case
    studies. | Violence in women—Political aspects—Case studies. |
    Feminism—Case studies.
Classification: LCC HQ1236 .G69 2021 (print) | LCC HQ1236 (ebook) |
    DDC 305.48/42—dc23
LC record available at https://lccn.loc.gov/2020048138
LC ebook record available at https://lccn.loc.gov/2020048139

———

To my Amma,
I was forged in your quiet ferocity,
dedication, and sacrifice.

my Appa,
Your empathy is my blood;
your fight for freedom my soul.

my Mohan Mama,
Thank you for the books, we miss you.

&

my dearest Che,
You are my everything,
the revolution, our future.

———

CONTENTS

RADICALIZING HER

INTRODUCTION

We are driving over small village roads built to hold the light tread of a bicycle; our vehicle toggles between potholes and brushing the edges of people's homes. My son plays a car game he has invented: when we pass slabs of erect gray concrete pockmarked with destruction he points, "Look at that one, Mom! Elephant or war?" He is hoping the answer is elephant and that one is lurking nearby for him to befriend.

We are in northern Sri Lanka, traveling swiftly over contested soil that was once liberated and is now, in 2018, occupied. We locate the home of Nayaki, a former guerrilla fighter, using the community positioning system: stopping every few feet for finger-pointing locals to guide us. It is next to the water tower and before the paddy fields.

Nayaki's daughter, a few years older than my son, opens the gate. Her mother is propped up by a small doorframe and one crutch. She smiles as the kids go out back where scattered chickens beckon.

In our meandering afternoon conversation her narrative moves as I have come to expect the narratives of fighters to move: twisting and turning, unsettling presumptions about her, or her politics. In the aftermath of battlefield life her stream of consciousness is at war with itself.

"I have no regrets in joining."

"The next generation shouldn't hear shelling."

"I miss the movement."

"I worry, now, with all the soldiers that my daughters are not safe."

"Women felt safe in the movement. Holding a gun."

Looking outward to the dust clouds filling the yard, she temporarily settles on a sentiment. "We must put the children forward, the children first."

The first time I listened to the lives of female fighters was ten years before my son was born, in the years when I was slowly tracing my own bloodlines across the ravaged island. From my earliest shared intimacies with these women I knew that the female fighter was deeply misunderstood and, worse, misjudged. The closer I came to women branded as extreme, the more normal their decisions seemed.

To the outside world, once she takes up arms the female fighter is simply a threat to be destroyed. To me, she takes up arms because she is the target. She is less extreme than she is mundane: every woman navigating layered circles of captivity.

For some, *Radicalizing Her* will be judged by its cover as an active action happening to a powerless her. The analysis of a narrow mind centers the fighter as an individual: she was feeling insignificant, she was pulled by a lover, she was brainwashed. Each assumption easily locates its gendered avatar in the weaknesses believed to be inherent to women.

Speaking from her days on the inside, Nayaki remembers, "There were so many reasons we joined the movement. Yes, as women it was a challenge to our culture, but mostly we wanted to stop the state from destroying us."[1] For her, the resistance is collective and gender-constitutive of a deep commitment.

The narratives I present of female fighters in Sri Lanka, Colombia, Syria, and elsewhere are drawn into the conversation with each other from inside the same spatial relationship to the state.

They were compiled over two decades (2001–2020) of time spent in conversation with hundreds of women—the patterns of traditional structured interviews were disrupted by the noise of a Bollywood dance party among former fighters, learning to build fiberglass fishing boats with cadres after a tsunami, sitting in the heavy silences of grieving families. Each story a plot point for mapping lives in the margins, spinning narrative threads that found each other and pulled at my own ties to violent histories.

Nayaki remembers the first moment she felt the force of oppression. "We were walking from school and my friend was struck by a sudden shelling." For most female fighters full moments pile on top of each other, seeds of consciousness taking root. As an activist friend reminds me often, "We are all political beings, still in formation."

An intrusive, insistent violence punctures every woman's life. As it violates, dismembers, and destroys she is expected to respond peacefully, carefully commodifying her trauma for others to rally around—the morally righteous path to political change. For more feminist-aligned thinkers, the female fighter is difficult to place. She absorbs each layer of trauma into her political thinking: not offering up a naked pain to sustain performative outrage in place of political change. She is conscious of patriarchy but positions it carefully inside a complex project for equality. She does not reject violence in the resistance that reaffirms her right to exist.

This book is a request to recalibrate: to reverse our view of the target, honing in on a violent state and the society it breeds.

These structures, the ones that restrain her movement, disappear when the view of the female fighter is myopic. They must be first brought into view, before they can be seen, studied, and dismantled. These are the forces that *radicalize her*. This is an urgent corrective to an erasure of the innate political power in every woman.

Moving from three sites of struggle (battlefield, stage, the streets) in the first section to three lines of defense (first, second, third) in the second, my goal in this text is to slowly reveal the myriad of external forces that threaten the existence of the woman who eventually takes up arms: the violent advances of state soldiers and the policy makers that hold the line; the role a woman plays in her own rape and the cultural constraints that hold her captive to trauma; the beatings at home and the guns on the streets that she will eventually fight to reclaim. Each encircling her, reinforcing the other—until she makes the radical choice to break through.

Radicalizing Her is rooted in the perspective of the female fighters who demand to be seen as political actors. While much has been rightly made of the surge of women in electoral politics, this text reclaims women's place in another form of political life: on the battlefield and in the streets. The erasure of the female fighter from narratives on gender and power is not only dangerous but also antifeminist.

Looking outward from her new positioning, Nayaki slowly places each crutch on the floor and remarks, "The children, our children, should not be afraid of anyone. They should live free." As a part of a lifelong project that took shape in the image of the female fighter, *Radicalizing Her* is open ended: offering no recommendations, only an exploration of new landscapes of political possibility. As the next generation of activist women lines up along the borders of contested political territories, the life histories of these female fighters offer new imaginaries for thought, and action, to break through, and rebuild.

Captured by a new context, Nayaki contemplates three choices: join the occupying military seeking guerrilla fighters, accept the handouts of chickens to raise, run for local political office against the active opposition of the men in her community. She looks dejected and returns to an earlier thought: "I miss the movement."

She switches suddenly to a choice that was entirely hers: an *iyyaku peyr* (or nom de guerre) chosen after completing six months of training in the jungle. "I chose Thaiya. I thought, nobody else is Thaiya. It is a strong name, don't you think?"

She pauses and murmurs softly, "Yes. I thought it was a good name for a very strong woman."

SECTION 1

SITES OF STRUGGLE

"The struggle happens in many places, in many different ways," Malathi would remind me. Back then, Malathi was a Tiger, a fighter, often found with boots caked in mud from a recent advance into army territory. Today she shouts orders to the other mothers protesting on stage, on the streets, for the return of their children, disappeared by the state.

Every political activist will eventually settle into her site of struggle, moving through different spaces to find her fit. The female fighter, the one that chooses violence, must also find her place inside of a movement.

For some cadres their lives on and off battlefields are a careful choreography between action and reflection that slowly constructs a new consciousness: the kind that advances our knowledge and expands our political imagination. For others, it is performance that offers, as a female combatant in Colombia would describe, "a catharsis and a reckoning" with the violence of their lives. The most visible will take the struggle to the streets, armed to defend their own right to exist.

In each of these sites, the female fighter will find both pain and political possibility.

CHAPTER 1

A BATTLEFIELD

ADVANCE AND RETREAT:
FRAGMENTS OF THE FEMALE FIGHTER

She is no longer a Tiger. Taken captive by the Sri Lankan government at the end of the war, she is an ex-combatant. For her and other women like her, detention is a halfway house for those nearly dead but counted among the living.

A government psychologist is among her only visitors. "How angry are you now?" he asks in broken Tamil. "Do you feel angry enough to throw a glass?"

"No," she later tells me. She doesn't feel.

She considers the question. Having been trained in combat, she thought that a glass thrown must be aimed at a target—but where would she direct her rage? At the guerrilla men with whom she shared a battlefield who now refuse her hand in marriage? At the soldiers who left her wishing she had joined her friends in a mass grave? At the NGO-funded "rehabilitation" teacher who places reams of fabric before her, demanding she stitch tiny yellow ducks? At him, the government-paid "neutral" psychologist?

He is waiting for her answer to assess her level of madness—not the source of her rage.

MOVEMENT

When the women I have known joined the Tigers, they set their lives in multidirectional motion. They would begin to move: from home to training camp, from a training camp to the base, from the base to the battlefield, to another battlefield, and another . . . until they were taken captive, detained, hidden away, and were suddenly still.

In any insurgency this movement is a continuum of conscious resistance. Memories of the aggressive mobility of war are marked with peaceful moments of reflection. Retreat can be read as a symbol of defeat, but it is also strategic—a central part of forward movement. The retreat is both tactical (to preserve resources) and thoughtful: an interlude for critical thinking, analysis, and recentering of political purpose (a space that activists off the battlefield often struggle to recognize as critical to movement building), before the next advance.

The most often repeated myth around the female fighter posits that her psyche—empty and untethered as it must be—was co-opted by the militancy, or "brainwashed." While many of the women I met over the years were indeed shown propaganda videos and participated in other forms of socialization into the movement, they describe their years on the battlefield, in both advance and retreat mode, as a deliberate participation in a process—one with access to a previously forbidden political space and where consciousness evolves slowly over time.

Through movement a political sense of self emerges. A fighter, a woman, willing and able to resist all forms of captivity, even the rebel leadership itself.

ADVANCE: THE MEMORY OF A MOVEMENT

When I wore the camouflage uniform and walked into the town
with a gun, there was some respect in the way everyone looked at
me. Now I go into the town with no gun, no uniform. Now people
turn their faces away when they see me, or they sneer at me. Like
a forged coin, I have no value.

—THAMIZHINI[1]

"Our madame," as the fighters called her, was middle-aged. Her
face twisted in ways that mimicked the austerity of the captured
female fighters, but Akila felt her physique was unfit for the demands of guerrilla warfare.[2]

When the government's madame spoke to the newly gathered Tiger cadres, she sneered, "We should have shot you all
in the jungle, so we don't have all these problems with you." It
might have affected them if they were not already so broken—
and Akila, was the only one who understood her English anyway.
From what Akila understood, deradicalization had two components: hard labor and spiritual guidance—the latter more jarring
than the former.

Akila rolls her eyes as she remembers the forced meditation.
The Buddhist monk sent to give spiritual guidance told her he advised the government to execute them, or "at least the high-level
cadres should have been killed." She wonders if they were paid to
come in and offer this enlightenment. The lucky ones were made
to stand in the sun for hours; others were charged with positivity
through the shock of an electric wire. Life on the inside, for Akila,
was "mentally torturous." Waiting for hours in the sun, manual
labor, even the occasional brute force of their madame. "It felt like
we were moving, and then we were still, paralyzed, trapped."

In total, there were approximately two thousand Tiger
women in detention. "In the early days of detention, the women

in the army were afraid of us. Maybe they didn't know that we were afraid of them." One day, our madame figured out that Akila spoke English and was skilled with computers and decided she would oversee data entry. This was in the fall of 2009, months after the final onslaught, and the data was names and ID numbers of Tiger cadres—each, living or dead, placed into the compact boxes of a 2006 version of Microsoft Excel.

The battlefield had changed, and Akila saw her role in front of a screen as the first (final) line of defense between the cadres and the state, which would extract information by any means necessary. The days passed in waiting, not for release but for a sighting of the TID (Terrorism Information Department) team that selected the ones who would face torture in exchange for information on terror.

One morning, a lower-level TID officer came to the computer. He asked Akila for a female cadre by name—was she there? Akila scrolled through the boxes in front of him; she had already made sure that the cadre in question was missing from her formatted cell. "Saving her was, at least, some form of resistance, even though we were captured—no?" Captive women move in slow, slight ways as they twist out of an iron grip.

Being captured, for most of the two thousand women on the inside with Akila, was a choice made from up against a wall of a brutal military assault. In the final days of the war, as indiscriminate shelling dismembered entire families, a loudspeaker played over the din of explosions. In garbled Tamil the demand came, "If you have been with the Tigers even one day, you must surrender to the army. We will find out if you have not surrendered." The announcement was seared into the memories of nearly every Tamil, repeated verbatim across hundreds of interviews: the moment when their faith was forcibly pulled from a movement and handed to the state.[3]

When defeat seemed a foregone conclusion the women cadres began to surrender. Akila arrived in detention determined to forget the old memories, her time in battle. As they stood still in long lines of forced labor, they were repeatedly told, "You lost the war. You have to move forward."

She considers the statement. "But this, this deradicalization, and how they treat us, it does not erase the memories. It only reminds us why we fought."

RETREAT: THE BOYS

Akila was born the year before me, in Jaffna, the hometown of my mother, my *amma*, at the northern tip of Sri Lanka. Amma was still there in the years before my birth and remembers celebrating her uncle, Pata, when he was first elected to the national government of Sri Lanka as a member of Parliament in 1977 to represent the island's ethnic minority, the Tamils.[4]

Pata ran at a moment when tensions were high. The majority ethnic group, the Singhalese, controlled the government and were lobbying to exclude Tamil-speaking citizens from government jobs. The process to limit Tamil admissions into university was already well under way. Peaceful protest by the Tamil minority had been met with military violence. A skilled orator, Pata had argued for the release of Tamil political prisoners, and his booming oration was quickly becoming the voice of a movement.

At the rally celebrating Pata's victory in the summer of 1977, my amma tells me that "the boys," as the nascent militancy was called then, cut their fingers before staining the middle of Pata's forehead with a thick red circle—strengthening his spiritual resolve to the Tamil cause for a separate state.

Less than a month later, the party's success left villages across the island in flames as anti-Tamil rioting spread to the capital city. "The boys" had grown into the Tamil Tigers and joined the growing demand for a Tamil homeland to be called Eelam.

At fourteen, and from afar, Pata was my hero and "the boys" were responsible for the revolution. At fourteen, Akila joined the Tigers.

ADVANCE: THE BATTLEFIELD

> *Though I primarily joined the movement because we were in a state of war, as a woman, I also thought of it as an opportunity to revolt and shatter the stereotypes of womanhood held by my family, and the community around me.*

> —THAMIZHINI[5]

When I meet Sandra, a senior commander now in Bogotá's branch of the FARC (Revolutionary Armed Forces of Colombia—People's Army), she has just been pardoned. A red headband pulls her hair back over her ears to reveal mouse-shaped gold earrings, each enlivened by a tiny red stone. With all the markings of the softly feminine, she pushes back the sleeves of a sweater adorned with a gold heart before she sits stiffly on the broken couch. A deep scar cuts across her left cheek and deepens as a dimple would, just slightly, when she speaks. She wants to be clear, from the outset: "I am not demobilized. I am still a fighter. A member of the FARC."[6]

Sandra is impressed that I know "Los Tigres." In the particular mythologies incubated inside the resistance, the Tigers held a special place. She has read about women in the Tigers and those in the PKK (Kurdistan Worker's Party): both made a separate state seem possible. "When I first joined the FARC there weren't a lot of other women joining," Sandra tells me. The decision required cutting ties from your family completely. "No family wants to be known as tied to the guerrillas."

As with the Tigers, entry into the FARC came with parallel initiations of political education and military training. I gently prod for her experience of military training, the rigor and difficulty. She responds with an insight into her own foot-soldier philosophy: "Everything in life is a process, isn't it?" People, she muses, are "animals of habit," and once you commit to life within a movement your body and mind adapt to a new way of being. Women, Sandra feels, are seen primarily for their role in the family. In fact, she tells me, "they are political subjects. Willing to work. Leaders, who draw people to them. Men are just not as good." She hesitates and mumbles an insincere sorry to the gentleman who has accompanied me.

Sandra doesn't believe she was socialized (or brainwashed) into the FARC. She is wary of theorists outside the movement. She considers the FARC "like a university," where the injustice she saw around her began to make sense. "Before joining the FARC I didn't just witness the killing of the few people, activists, who wanted social change—there were mass killings."

It was Sandra herself who recruited more women into the FARC. While she often relayed the FARC's rules that spoke to gender equity, she cautioned them that this was not always the reality. As the number of women cadres grew there were internal conversations. "We asked them not to underestimate women's capabilities." Some men understood; others didn't. In her own battalion Sandra is most proud of having cultivated political perspectives. "I was the one who helped the women who needed to build their political stature."

RETREAT: THE FEMALE FIGHTER

My mother pleaded with me not to go back to the island she escaped after her mother's death. "I won't sleep worrying about your safety," Amma would say. She felt certain that, as a Tamil, I was at risk. Filled with a fresh-out-of-college headiness, I went anyway.

A few weeks before my return, a funeral caravan carried Pata's body across the now Tiger-controlled territories. I was too late. The questions for him I had carried with me across continents would go unanswered. In between the pages of rambling reflections in my journal, I carefully folded the yellowed pages of Pata's local obituaries alongside the colorful artwork of Tamil children I had just met.

On my arrival in Sri Lanka, I would stay only one night in the capital before heading directly into villages inside Tiger territory. By this time the group controlled nearly a quarter of the island: Eelam was real. I would be working with young Tamil women in the war zone, teaching English in a children's home inside a church. I was drawn to Nirmala, an eleven-year-old girl with perfectly plaited hair, who shared my amma's first name.

Like many of the other children, Nirmala was not an orphan, but "because of the war, this orphanage is the only place my amma felt I would be safe." Each child in the orphanage was given a small box for items that were special to them, neatly tucked away in cubbies beside their bunk beds. It was on one of our first afternoons together that Nirmala gingerly pulled out a photo of her elder sister in fatigues, afraid to crease it. "This was the last time I saw her," she tells me. "It was the day she joined the Tigers."

The faded image of a woman grasping a rifle framed by foliage stood in sharp contrast to the role I was taught Tamil women were meant to play: demure, modest, blending into the background of most of my childhood memories. It was the first time that shards of my own perceptions of violence, and revolution, glared back at me. From up close, I could suddenly see the complicated political lives of Tamil women in the resistance.

In one of the many ensuing years—they blurred together over time—I remember sitting in the dust of a refugee camp with female fighters from the Tigers, chatting about a boy, some object of affection. An elderly uncle approached slowly and smiled widely revealing a sparse collection of betel-leaf-stained teeth. He had come to tell me that he knew my grandmother. Looking back to his wife, he said, "She is an activist, she is here to help. Just like Devi."

It was then that I learned who my grandmother really was. That immediately after giving birth to my aunt she was asked to canvas in remote villages, engorged breasts and all, for Pata's political campaign. That she felt it her duty to serve the Tamil people. That she was a diminutive figure who could make Pata cower when she fiercely argued with him on his policies. That at the same 1977 rally for Pata my mother remembers, from amidst "the boys" emerged Devi. The only woman to reach up to her brother's forehead to mark her own contribution to the struggle, with blood.

And it was only then that I learned how my mother's amma died in 1978—from the typhoid she contracted as one of the only women willing to serve food to the untouchable refugees fleeing the first flares of war. Devi, the men agreed, was the reason Pata was in power.

It was five years after Devi's death that Mathivathani Erambu, a young Tamil student, would begin her protest in her own bid for power—demanding that the Tigers include women in their ranks.

ADVANCE: THE BATTLEFIELD

On the edge, Ms Militancy bayed for more blood.
Vending vengeance, she made a bomb
Of her left breast and blew up the blasted city.
Long after that land had turned to ashes,
The rest of her plucked breast bled.

——MEENA KANDASAMY[7]

Ex-combatants and close affiliates of the Tigers knew that there was an assessment of new recruits—a kind of 1990s guerrilla version of the evaluation apps to identify high-performing consultants in the business world—before they were placed inside the organization.

Akila was found to be intelligent and was sent to study English in 1993 before joining her battalion on the battlefield at the age of nineteen. "In the early days I would cry, it was so different, and I was afraid the animals would kill me." She remembers thinking that "the older women, the ones who had been there ten years already, they really seemed to like it."

Over the years some fighters I met would speak of loss on the battlefield, most often the friends hastily left in the jungle. Akila spoke with clarity of the feeling she had when she went to war. "When I was young, I wanted to do some extraordinary things; I believed I could." She describes feeling equal, feeling free. "I hate the concept of women, under men, in anything. I will not be a slave to my husband, or the state." The battlefield as a forced gender equalizer is something I would hear again, and often—some longing for it many years after they returned to civilian life.

Even inside the movement, the women had to fight. "There were, of course, many hardships. We were not used to the physical toll this would have on our bodies. We woke early, at 4 a.m."

Before they made it to the battlefield, their dedication was tested, over and over again.

"I was ready to go to battle and I was told I wasn't ready." Akila was adamant and joined the next advance, a carefully planned ambush of a military checkpoint.

"When we won, I was thrilled. Suddenly, everything seemed possible."

RETREAT: ON VIOLENCE

On the question of violence the tendency of contemporary political discourse to parse the world into "for" and "against" camps obscures our view of the female fighter. An understanding of motivations to fight will be read as condoning violence, oppressive agendas given the upper hand by the moral imperative to condemn it. In the end, the false dichotomy serves only as a salve for the selective consciousness of the audience and conversations on political violence are encircled inside an echo chamber. Violence, for me, and for the women I chronicle in this book, is simply a political reality.

In her iconic 1970 essay *On Violence*, Hannah Arendt asks that we "raise the question of violence in the political realm"[8]— that we examine the relationship between violence and political power. She celebrates the nonviolent resistance of the American civil rights sit-ins but condemns any semblance of violence in the resistance. Scholars have noted a kind of reverence in Arendt's work of the masculine performance of power and her overt exclusion of women from this space.[9] Violence, for Arendt, is antithetical to power.

Contemporary feminist thinkers like Rebecca Solnit understand violence through the feminist organizing principle of gender equality. Violence, for Solnit, is ultimately about the desire of men to dominate and control women.[10]

Neither analysis acknowledges the existence, or even the possibility, of the women for whom violence is a form of resistance—the only option to access power. The impulse to condemn violence in the resistance (while implicitly condoning the violence of the state) is a moral imperative that matters very little to the lives this violence permeates.

Nonviolent protest in the face of state violence (reliant on mobilizing the moral conscience of others) has long been the prescribed, progressive pathway to political change. To access this space, violated women are most often expected to wear trauma as an identity card, their injuries used to incite outrage. A woman who slings a gun across her chest, resisting the commodification of her trauma, is jarring to a liberal sense of self.

A foundational Tamil thinker would note that as young men and women began joining the Tigers, "the Tamil youth looked around and saw no allies. They had only themselves to rely on. They had no choice but to take up arms. The violence of the violated is never a matter of choice, but a symptom of choicelessness."[11]

In 1969, Leila Khaled, a member of the Popular Front for the Liberation of Palestine, was the first woman to hijack an airplane, diverting TWA Flight 840 en route to Rome. A few years later, in Oakland, California, Elaine Brown became the first female militant to chair the Black Panther Party. In 1983, Mathavani Erambu vowed to fast until death, protesting the treatment of the Tamil minority in Sri Lanka, before eventually becoming one of the first female cadres in the Liberation Tigers of Tamil Eelam.

Though the female fighter is often seen as an anomaly, women have gone on to make up nearly 30 percent of militant movements worldwide. Historically these women have been deeply misunderstood. I have heard the female recruit to violence described as a "deviant" or "sociopath." Sometimes, in disguise, she "masquerades as a migrant." She is one of "those people" who is to blame for both her poverty and the poor ethical codes it creates. She is "antisocial" rather than a product of society's deep inequality. As in Mary Shelley's *Frankenstein*, the Monster is born from the minds of her makers. She is both their creation and their enemy.

In the United States today, Black women are increasingly purchasing permits to carry concealed weapons, as are their counterparts in the alt-right. Colombian women who fought in the FARC are refusing to lay down their arms, and women in Pakistan are both enlisting in the national army and supporting the Taliban. Each, in their own way, engages in the "violence of the violated."

In recent years violent women have begun to enter the public consciousness, tinted with the sensationalism of the Western media. From Hasna Atboulahcin, the suicide bomber in Paris, to Tashfeen Malik, a shooter in San Bernadino, California, we wait for the moment of extremism and scramble to look backward for meaning and motivation. An inability to grapple with the ways in which violence has intersected with these women's lives leaves us without answers—for the questions that were asked too late.

ADVANCE: AN INTERVIEW

The portrait of a female fighter is difficult to paint with soft strokes. She is used to being seen through hardened eyes, and she will show a hardened soul. Janani was my third interview that afternoon, on one of my earliest trips to a village on the Eastern shores, and my first with a woman who took up arms.[12]

The heat was oppressive in the tiny room held tenuously together by metal scraps. Earlier that day she and the other ex-Tigers had used the space for classes in carpentry. Eyes lined with fatigue, Janani sits across from me. She settles into the wide curve of a plastic garden chair, constructed to provide only the semblance of support.

She looks quietly, expectantly, suspiciously, waiting to be probed for the suffering, past and present. When I first met a female fighter, I didn't know yet that an interview could be a conversation but was more likely an opportunity: a chance for her to articulate objections and a reminder of my own vulnerability to err. An interview, at best, is the chance for a story to be told and, at worst, another interrogation.

I fidget with my scarf—constantly trying to arrange it in its most conservative form. She is tall, with long black hair, and eyes that turn up ever so slightly. She looks like me. An inescapable bridge forms over the space between us. What would I have done . . . if I were her?

My inner monologue is quickly silenced as she demands to know the nature of my research. "I am tired of questions for the sake of questions!" More importantly, she is plain tired.

She narrates her own life as a parallel track alongside the violence that shaped it. She begins her story in the middle of her mother's. "My amma was disturbed, I think after my father left to fight. My job was to raise my siblings." Life as a child was divided into categories of challenges: a small home, no running water, people were always sick. She points to her missing fingers: "I was cooking for my siblings when the stove exploded."

Interspersed within her civilian experience were armed intrusions. The military, and its accompanying arrests, torture, and harassment, were always a peripheral presence in her consciousness. "The government soldiers were always around; we avoided them. I had heard of the Tigers, and I was glad someone was fighting for us." An entire world away, the faint soundtrack of my own childhood also included the Tigers: they inhabited her reality and my imagination.

Janani was eighteen when the woman recruiter, a fighter, entered her classroom. She wore a stern expression and fatigues that fell loosely along the contours of her body. "I was asked to join the Tigers, for my people. I could not refuse.

"The training was hard; it was difficult for me. But we fought for a better life for the Tamil people. Everyone deserves better than this . . ." She waves her hand as if to capture her existence off the battlefield. She is constantly harassed by the army as an ex-fighter. Not because she was one, but because missing fingers on her hand suggest she might have been.

"I have my children to consider now, but yes, I would fight again." Not yet a mother myself at this point, the statement surprised me. Even motherhood, a powerfully transformative force, faltered in the face of her dedication to the cause.

It was only a chance overlap of luck and privilege that carved an escape tunnel out of this place for me. There was not even a generation between us, and I wondered where a different twist of fate might have positioned the two of us.

RETREAT: THE BOXES

One evening in New York, when I am recently divorced and well acclimated to motherhood, two Tamil uncles transfer history from a basement in New Jersey to my apartment. History has often been handed over to me by the uncles. A trolley helps bear the weight, and the deposit is made. We go out for Thai food. Tamils love Thai food.

When I return, the boxes spill over, occupying the small space I worked hard to eke out for myself and my son. They tempt me in the mornings and taunt me before bed. They threaten to overwhelm me. Occasionally a New York summertime brown bug finds its way into the boxes. Stuffed in between the VHS Tiger recruitment videos are bent photos of Tamil women in bell-bottoms protesting outside the White House. Hidden in the pages of grandstanding men's speeches is the stenciled artwork of a female fighter. Binders are overflowing with letters, appeals to humanity signed by long-dead dignitaries. Tissue paper–thin political pamphlets calling for revolution that once circulated covertly in occupied villages now lay still.

> *It is as if some material traces had returned from this departed world, traces of moments that were the most private and the least often expressed. Moments when people were taken by surprise or pained or at least feigned being so. The archive preserves these moments at random, chaotically.*
>
> —ARLETTE FARGE[13]

A thick booklet, emblazoned with the insignia of the Tigers, is a rare archival find: a collection of speeches by the leader, Vellupillai Prabhakaran. On International Women's Day in 1992, he cited the dual struggle for Tamil women against Tamil patriarchy and a racist state.[14]

The boxes are a seductive black hole to lose myself in a singular passion. The materials are equal parts enabler and validation to those obsessed with the cause of one community.

In stolen moments I pull pieces to read, to translate: a stack of papers to strengthen the female fighter's platform. By then, I knew to scour for the markings of, and about, Tamil women on this historical content. Even within a single box, it is clear that the earliest history of a movement notes the shift in perceptions of women's political potential in Tamil society.

After my son fusses his way to sleep one night, I sift through the contents of the box closest to the couch. Inside an early media publication an elderly political supporter of the Tigers writes:

> How the Tamil woman, who was a docile, meek, peace loving member of the Tamil society turned out to be such a courageous, bold, and sacrificing person offering herself to fight injustice and to save the Tamil nation, is really unbelievable. But it's true.[15]

I feel the acute burden of materials that are both meaningful, and without concerted effort, meaningless.

ADVANCE: WHY WOMEN FIGHT

Like the women in the Tigers, Sandra first revisits her connection to a cause before reflecting on her positioning as a woman. After countless hours with female combatants, I know that budding seeds of consciousness form in women much earlier than we look for them.

Sandra recalls, "I remember being ten, maybe eleven years old. I would hear the sound of rattling on the street outside and jump under the bed. I was sure it was the soldiers." She later explains that often it was the early morning carts laden with corn to sell bumping along the stone pathways. Though temporarily inaccurate, the fear remains rational.

Her adolescence was marked by the moments she takes up public, political space. "I was always socially conscious. I was the president of my student council in high school and was the head of the community council when I graduated."

Nevertheless, she followed the path expected of her, taking a position in a government office before she intended to begin law school, committed to working for change on the inside. "We knew the government was rich; they were corrupt. But then there was the huge deficit and everyone got fired. I looked for a job everywhere."

Sandra began to sell small items, batteries, clocks, on the streets, wandering farther away from the familiar neighborhoods where she grew up. Eventually she entered the militarized zones. The camps she had heard of, the guerrillas she had never met.

"The FARC was so close to what I believed, inside. I wanted to be a part of this FARC, the one that fought for social justice."

When I meet Akila for the first time, she insists on placing the order herself at the Cosi cafe on Fifteenth and K: an egg-and-pepper croissant with a Coke. She is free to do so now that she is deradicalized.

I admire the yellow swirls around the sequins of her *salwar kameez*, a faltering attempt at a soft entrance into a hard life. She ignores the remark and begins. "I am disgusted, now, with what politics has become." She sits down in a corner of the café just a few blocks from the White House that has just welcomed Donald Trump.

As she deconstructs her croissant, looking for the peppers to add life to a dull sausage, Akila explains her choice to me before I can ask why. "There were aerial bombardments from the government. Every day. I was a child, I was scared, and I knew we had to fight them."

A response so simple as to render the question stupid. Her sister had joined the movement a few years earlier, as a member of the reconnaissance team. When she returned home in fatigues, "she appeared to me as so brave. This was attractive. I was attracted to that."

To Akila, in the unencumbered clarity of youth, it was less a decision to join a movement than an urgency to chase the army out of her home village so they could live peacefully.

Two years later, I would share a coffee in London with Adele Balasingham, popularly known as simply "Auntie," who married into the movement, eventually training and organizing the women in the Tigers. To convince her of my own credibility, when I ask her about the motivations of female cadres I follow quickly with, "Of course, I understand it's very complex."

She pauses, running her fingers slowly across the marble of the table as if to smooth the stone. "Is it?" Silence.

RETREAT: THE MYTH OF THE FEMALE FIGHTER

I had spent the first two summers of graduate school working with young Tamil women in Sri Lanka, many of whose lives were lived in and around the Tigers. I saw this as political work for a cause, separate from the intellectual research I was meant to be doing. My advisors wanted me to study (objectively) big politics: ethnic conflict and civil wars. Activism and women simply were not a part of that—both too soft to contribute to the backbone of a hard science.

Early on in my study of revolution, one text, *Why Men Rebel*,[16] seemed to be the subtext to all other studies of pathways into guerrilla movements. Even inside a discipline that insists on an adherence to precise science, arguments of why "people" joined rebellions were (secretly) coded to refer to men.

The corrective to this wasn't solely identifying patriarchy as the perpetrator, nor was it an oversight that was limited to the academy. The myths surrounding female fighters are most visible as they swirl around those women whose faces make it into the glare of media.

To see women as political actors, in complex, violent ways, still requires accessing a kind of otherworld. Myths are often understood to be ambivalent or ambiguous in their very nature— they offer multiple meanings to be subjectively extracted. The mythologies surrounding women have the ability to be both liberatory (the superhero-like figure of Malala) or oppressive (the powerless victim of sexual violence). In their bid to make the not yet known intellegible, myths are constantly reproduced, spawning mini-myths that themselves fertilize ground for spreading dangerous political narratives.

> Recall how you had gazed, in the nacreous light,
> at her speed, her allure, then begged to gain the same
> mystic skills—to wage war underseas, to ignite
> oceans with a single spell. Remembrance reclaims
> you now, oblivion blossoms into shame.
>
> —KARTHIKA NAIR[17]

As reductive mini-biographies emerge ("she liked Harry Potter, wore jeans, and listened to Coldplay"), myths about women participating in violence shape public opinion and the narratives that try to understand them—from the academy to public discourse.

The common myths shrouding the female fighter are born of deep-seated beliefs about gender more broadly and can be lumped into four oppressive myths: women are more peaceful than men by nature; women are brainwashed into militant movements; women join movements because of the men in their lives; empowerment programming can save the female fighter.

Fantastical myths of a "liberatory" nature are equally problematic. Photographers look to capture her through (their own) juxtaposition of femininity: pink manicured nails on an AK-47.

Artists in South Asia turn to the goddesses—providing the female fighter with the arms missing in the lives of their worshippers. Cartoons that can never fully sketch the violence of graphic moments outline a woman who is equal parts sensual and fierce. A new incarnation of Wonder Woman is idolized by girls everywhere for the projected power of femininity, ignoring the politics of an actress who supports the violent occupation of Palestinian lands.

> It is always difficult to describe a myth; it does not lend itself to being grasped or defined; it haunts consciousnesses without ever being posited opposite them as a fixed object.
>
> —SIMONE DE BEAUVOIR[18]

Even in the fantasy, she is captive. Each of the liberatory superpowers offered will tether her to a limited imagination. The power of invisibility allows the feminists in search of missing nonviolent voices to disappear her; superhuman strength will offer her the physical abilities of masculinity that leave her unsuitable for marriage; invulnerability will place her outside the safety net of donors, charities, and empowerment advocates alike—she is neither the good victim to be saved nor the peaceful political agent to be supported.

When I meet Akila again, a few years later, I mention that many people think female fighters have been brainwashed. She smiles, slowly. I wonder if perhaps something has gotten lost in translation. I ask again and she replies, "Yes, I understood. I was not brainwashed. I was motivated—to fight."

CHAPTER 2

THE STAGE

The Role of Rape

CENTER STAGE: TUNIS

When we rescue a girl from ISIS, Mohammed tells me over a tiny cappuccino in Tunis, she must sign a document that reads: "I agree that I am now a member of an organization that is against violence & terrorism. Tunisia is a country of peace."

Then, she can be saved.

The tribunal in Tunis had been heralded as the first of its kind. One where the use of rape and sexual torture of women by state forces would be revealed for what it was—the violent suppression of political dissent.

As I travel to Tunisia, the courts in London are flooded with requests for asylum from Sri Lanka; the Tamil community is considering a tribunal for accountability. The judges fear, several Western lawyers told me, that Tamil women are exaggerating claims of rape to receive asylum. A Tamil organization in need of expert advice will send me the medicolegal reports, proof of sexual torture, of twenty-six women.

When I arrive at the address of the much-heralded Tunisian tribunal, I find the building itself has none of the markings of grandeur one expects of places of historic significance. Its bland structure implies that justice is just another administrative task.

The hesitancy of women to take the stand emerges in different ways: they cite their children's concerns at inviting public shame; a conflict with their husbands' political interests; the failures of their own memory.

"When it comes out, the story is in bits and pieces," a tribunal officer tells me. "They recall being taken from their homes, the first part. But it falls apart when you ask, then what happened?"[1]

Sometimes the track of their testimonies jumps to the hospital, other times it derails into the relationship formed with a prostitute cohabiting a detention cell. Some women would enter the building with a complaint of sexual assault only to deny the very same violence as they take the stand, their secret center stage. "At the prospect of revealing the incident," most of the officers agree, "she is suddenly overcome by shame."

Inside a sterile room where beige fades to grey, I sit with Saba. When we meet in 2015, she has already given her testimony publicly. In her performance the man, the accused, never appears. Saba has returned to the building for support. She is uncertain of the role of the tribunal: "I'm not sure how you take this witness statement to a global audience. How do you make clear the disparity of power between the people and the state?"[2] She knows I have worked with female militants and asks me to explain her daughter Miriam's perspective—to her.

Miriam was born in the shadow of her mother's activism and came of (teen) age in the Jasmine Revolution. Even after her cold articulation of the facts, Saba still felt the ghost of the state police, inside her and on top of her. Her organs ached with the most natural of movements, sagging skin layered around the scarring that grew darker over time. Miriam was young then. Saba was young then. Listening to her, I wondered, how does rape age inside of women as the world around them moves on unbothered?

> *Did we know we were gradually falling apart?*
> *Disintegrating into pieces. That's the last stage. When*
> *there are bits that could be held together, but no skin to*
> *make them hold.*
>
> —QUENTIN ANA WIKSWO[3]

The state, pulling justification from repressive regimes elsewhere, will argue that Saba's detention was administrative—a matter of procedure, not punishment. As the testimonies pile into a pattern, they suggest otherwise.

Miriam remembers trying to identify the offense, clarify the purpose of her sudden absence during her mother's days inside. Had she crossed a cultural barrier as a woman or a political blockade as an activist? Her mother was captured for an act of dissent, but the uniformed men who raped her reminded her she was a woman.

"Either way, she shouldn't have left us—her children. After all, she is a mother first."[4] The normalcy of built-in mother-daughter angst set against the backdrop of extreme circumstances.

Saba's anger, now, fades in the shadow of her daughter's frustration. "I think my daughter wants to join the Islamist group, in the mountains, that is fighting against the government," she tells me. As elsewhere, the violence that has been formative to the state's history, its sense of self, will shape the identities of the generations that grow beneath it.

Saba rarely sees Miriam's face anymore. It is hidden, behind the screen of her laptop. Decorative stickers have been carefully placed around the luminescent apple—Arabic graffiti and the outline of an AK-47.

"I cannot understand her choice."

Miriam asks why her mother waits in line, with other victims, outside the tribunal in Tunis. "Why go back inside, why speak her truth to the state that tortured her for resisting?" Miriam asks.

"I cannot understand her choice."

Mohammed was remarkably unconcerned with his problematic positioning on these struggles, later explaining to me that given the secrecy and shame that accompanies sexual violence in Tunisian society, only the mother can influence her daughter not to make a bad decision. "Women, you know, are considered our whole society's dignity." When they have been raped he feels their dignity is affected and dismisses the choices of young women as political. "She might just rather be dead than have her dignity affected."

A few weeks after we meet, Saba and Miriam would be separated: the mother whose peaceful protest ended in violence, a daughter following a political vision that begins there.

I am just back in New York when the package arrives—the unassuming black shoebox stuffed with information on the sexual torture of Tamil women. I do not open it. I put it under the bed.

THE FINAL ACT

When we perform for the people, it is like the Greek theater.
This is their catharsis.

—OFELIA MEDINA[5]

Ofelia Medina was an actress before she was a rebel, a rebel before she was an activist. In 1990, when the rape of indigenous women by Mexican government soldiers was commonplace, she famously trekked for nearly twelve hours through underbrush to reach the Zapatista hideout—at first armed only with her walking stick. In Chiapas, the faces of Zapatista women were masked by bandanas, and a jagged gun barrel draped over their bodies: they articulated political demands for the good of the community and held their weapons close to protect themselves. When I met her, decades later, Ofelia had chosen the stage as her site of struggle: a space to explore the nationwide plague of femicide in Mexico through the story of one mother.

Walking through the tree-lined streets of the Coyoacán, I step over lazy slivers of sunshine. As I open the theater door slowly, natural light casts a spotlight on the dark stage. Startled mid-scene, Ofelia shields her eyes to look up at me: the entrance is too bright. Ofelia plays the mother; the other actress, the daughter. The four walls are entirely black. As I grasp for a seat they return to the scene, swaying toward and away from each other: in conversation and contestation.

Holding her daughter's head in her palm, the mother splays her fingers to cover the entirety of her scalp: her only defense against the impending threat to the life she created. "Please go," she begs her daughter. "Leave him." She speaks softly, indicating the "he" is close. The daughter wears a white skirt, long enough for modesty's sake and thin enough to breathe—a luxury allowed only in her husband's absence.

As the scenes play out inside a blackened box, the figure of the man is an absence, his presence detected only by the reaction of the women's bodies. His entrance is felt when Ofelia falls; he is the force pushing the mother aside. Impact is spotlighted with intent.

Invisible children are hushed; the daughter twirls her hair into a knot and pulls the skirt over her quivering knees. What lies beneath it is already his conquest. She sits in front of the children born of his semen and her blood, offering up a shaky smile to shield them from their father.

> *We are hundreds of girls. You will have to slit each one's throat or*
> *sharpen us to watch over your memory. Give us knives. We have*
> *to think. Vaults. We are mines throbbing. The sky has the most*
> *beautiful legs. We are perfect. Use us and damage us.*
>
> —DOLORES DORANTES[6]

It is this moment, just before the daughter's inevitable death, that I have come to Mexico to understand. She will soon be the missing dimension inside this diorama of death. Where rape desires domination, femicide seeks extermination. The escalation from the former to the latter, the entire neighborhoods left womanless, can only be explained in dismembered fragments: the Narcos, the Catholic Church, culture, machismo, corruption, the plundering greed of US interventions. Sergio González Rodríguez describes the town where body parts accumulate. "In Ciudad Juárez . . . people become dehumanized. Society itself acquires an asocial status: its members feel disconnected from it."[7]

Off stage, the mother played by Ofelia is in fact Marisela Escobedo Ortiz, a woman shot outside a government building in Chihuahua, mid-protest. She is buried in a dark wooden coffin, alongside the beaten body of her sixteen-year-old daughter. "When we perform," Ofelia tells me, "women will come to the theater and scream, wail. This is beyond crying. This is the only way to express the pain."

Three years after the summer Marisela was killed, a woman boarded the morning bus in Ciudad Juárez in the midst of an interminable wave of femicide in the state. Instead of her bus fare, she pulled a gun from her purse. After she shot and killed the bus driver, the woman, known as "Diana the Hunter," sent a note:

> We can no longer be silent in the face of these acts that enrage us. We were victims of sexual violence from bus drivers working the maquila night shifts here in Juárez. Nobody does anything to protect us. That's why I am the instrument that will take revenge for many women.[8]

THE REHEARSAL

The coffee shop in central London offers the opportunity to sit still amid the activity that surrounds you. A place that melts away into the mundane. Latha meets me here, straight from the jungle theater of war for her third (and not final) rehearsal.[9]

Her white gauzy dupatta scarf hangs like an oversized appendage from her borrowed bomber jacket. It is the only part of the costume that's hers, and the only one she doesn't remove. She tugs off the furry beanie that sits awkwardly perched on the edge of her head and smooths her hair back into a perfect part—framing the red circle on her forehead that wavers between remembrance and resistance.

She is suspicious of her latte, a rich woman's milk coffee, but smiles warmly when she looks up at me. I want nothing more than to stay in the silence of this moment.

She starts with the circles. The Sri Lankan army surrounded the huddle of civilians that found each other in the muddy marathon through the jungle to escape the bombings. The group was tightly knit, the soldiers heavily armed. She unknowingly inserts her own numbers into the spreadsheet tracking a darkly divisive numbers game. Government math made civilian casualties magically disappear as advocates for international intervention into the bombardment tried to trace signs of life in safe zones that once held tens of thousands of breathing bodies. I have always thought that an inevitable statistical bias should err on the side of the damned.

Latha's numbers are estimates from the middle of trauma: "Maybe two hundred, two hundred and fifty," she thinks were in this inner circle. "We were placed in groups of twenty," to control a crowd on the verge of collapse. "We were all, men and women, asked to remove our clothes—even my underskirt." She breaks eye contact, a Tamil woman's instinct to succumb to shame. The underskirt, I was told as a teenager, is the last layer of protection. A flimsy guard against the transparent threat of immodesty.

As the final curtain of their collective humanity fell, the army advanced. "They moved through us, into the middle of the circle." In this new formation choreographed out of chaos, she and the others were asked to walk slowly around the military huddle. "They already knew," she explains, "that we didn't have any arms." The men were recaptured and taken away, so that only the women remained. Then they were raped.

> *Territory with no harbor, land with no stopping place, body with empty heart. Place drained of blood we are all yours running. All running to enter you . . . we place ourselves tidily like soldiers or jewels.*
>
> —DOLORES DORANTES[10]

Latha had expected questions, an interrogation—but I had long since stopped asking women for the gory details of rape. I don't need to know. In the global plague of violence against women, the woman who pretends she is raped is an anomaly, driven by desperation in different ways. For the women I have worked with, rape is not a threat. It is an inevitability. When sex is the weapon wielded by the state, rage festers in the wounds of its victims. In my silence, Latha pauses, redirects. She remembers visiting her daughter, Kala, the week after she joined the Tigers— nearly a decade ago now.

Latha had not told her husband and traveled alone by bus to the training camp, where a young female cadre respectfully greeted her. "Amma, please have a seat, and wait." She remembers her daughter's face, the stubborn set of her eyes that she recognized but a distance that was new. "Amma," Kala said, "I have thought about it, this is what I have to do. If we don't fight, we will never be safe." She refused to come home.

I would meet Kala two years after she last saw her mother. She has been in hiding. Her entire life is a secret to ensure her survival.[11]

When she surrendered, she was placed in the back of the van. Kala describes a dark so enveloping she felt it. A metal chair so cold it broke through threadbare cotton. "I heard only the sound of my own shivers." She remembers lifting her dupatta, only a thin veil of protection, over her head.

She was taken to the camp they had heard of. The one for female fighters only, blocked to all except the drivers. A doctor sent in would later confirm that drivers were often told to take the girls "for entertainment" and then return them.

The doctor is forbidden to look for the rape Kala won't reveal. "I saw bullet injuries, shrapnel, obstructed bowels, broken bones badly set, lung wounds, but I could not conduct any other examinations."

Kala remembers the fighter who tried to leave, every single night. When she couldn't escape, she would scream. Deep, guttural screams that came from a place that no doctor, nor any of us, could see.

———————

Months later, the US government would feign temporary blindness when the satellite imagery revealed the chakra-like circles of Tamil women, each rape taking place on its spiked edges. From the vantage point of a drone, Tamil men would be reduced to scattered outlying dots: a captive audience. The young, unmarried women were transported separately. They are the missing data, the disappeared.

"I have a lot of trouble with excess bleeding now, but I think this must be menopause," Latha muses. It is the manifest destiny of a woman's hormones to bear the burden of blame for forces far more destructive to the inner workings of the female body. It was a local doctor who helped her escape, citing a medical emergency to facilitate her handoff to relatives in the United Kingdom.

Latha has heard that the details of her life are floating somewhere between her village roads and the information superhighway. "I hear that my story was discussed in Geneva. I don't know what it will achieve. Haven't the Tamils been appealing to the United Nations for years?" They have.

After a year in London, she finally picks up the phone to start making phone calls back home trying to locate her daughter. She shouts so they can hear her voice; they whisper so nobody else hears theirs. She learns that her mother has died in the camp where she left her and her daughter is disappeared. She was denied the screams beside bodies taken from her.

She tells me that sometimes when the phone rings with a request for an interview, she doesn't want to answer any more questions.

She shakes her head. "Sometimes I think this, telling the story, this is torture."

PERFORMING RAPE

The pristine white roof of London's ExCel Center billows in its own circuslike tent. Underneath, the show goes on. For members of a trade or tribe, one can find everything from the newest accounting software to carefully constructed mosquito-repellant clothing for aid workers to survive among survivors.

This afternoon, the ExCel Center is hosting the Global Summit to End Sexual Violence, a lively arcade of endless options to end rape. One might collapse into a colorful beanbag to join the hackathon, purchase a traditional basket to "uplift the voices of survivors," or wander through some genuinely thoughtful discussions on wartime rape until the gravitational pull of Angelina Jolie's presence draws audiences to gawk.

He shouldn't have been in the audience. But so few of his choices were his own anymore. The well-meaning white network that caught him as he fell now shepherds him through a new safe zone—one with its own hidden threats to what is left of his life. In one small breakout session, his trauma is being played out on stage.

His story, "Torture Victim 3," follows the narrative arc of most victim-survivors who wished they were still called by their birth names, chosen in consultation with the stars. The climax comes before the character. It begins with rape. As the story is told, his character is fleshed out to establish innocence.

He is passionate about a just cause, though never violent in his pursuit of it. He supported the Tigers, but never held a gun. His civil civilian innocence is highlighted to play up the genocidal glint in the eye of the state.

The actor on stage is short, black, and British. Every fiber of his being comes to life as he reads the script. His reenactment of another man's rape is charismatic. The journalist who brought him, Torture Victim 3, to bear witness to himself is a white woman.

Positioning herself beside him, she is determined to be allowed on his journey as the necessary emotional support for his undiagnosed mental state. He walks out of the audience just before the part where he is tortured.

SHIFTING SCENES

When I was a child the aunties often asked, with the usual tinge of judgment, "Is Nimmi your full name?" Nimmi is short for Nirmala, my mother's name. The nickname is my legal name, and only once did I come across another Nimmi.

She was my age, Sri Lankan, and an actress in London. We became friends in 2009, the year some say the conflict ended in Sri Lanka. We were both, Nimmi and I, interviewing Tamil women seeking safety in the United Kingdom. Nimmi shares one of her interviews with me. The first time the pages of the PDF pop open, I have to close them. For weeks the file sits heavy, tucked away behind the tabs of more benign documents.

I decide to print Siva's story, the tiniest offering of respect. On paper I read her testimonial over and over.[12]

Siva's eyes close for just a minute.[13]

She is on the streets of Jaffna. Sari pleats fall loose around her slippers, and her freshly washed hair is tied back at the nape of her neck. She is adorned with only simple gold bangles. Looking down, her eyes trace lines in the red earth.

When she performs, the customary thick silk costume is tightly tucked into musical belts and bells to ensure rhythmic precision. Two eyes are widened with black lines beneath a bejeweled third, her lips stained bright red. Here, every step she takes is heard, every movement she makes is sensual.

With her culture's blessing, Siva demands to be seen. She even catches the camera's eye. She owns the stage.

She opens her eyes, back in the moment.

"I am not a terrorist" is the line they want. She tries to repeat it. In this role, they find her unconvincing.

The set is sparse: one rubber mat and a pillow. Rusted bars are the only way in and out of this set. A single metal pipe and white sand make up the remaining props.

The soldiers ask her to dance for them. They ask for her autograph, on an image of her former self and an admission of guilt that will sentence her to death in a foreign language. Here she performs daily. "I take a bath in front of them, watching me, what I am doing, all the time," the transcript reads.

"The problem," the interrogator tells her, "is you are beautiful, you know? You understand?"

The scene plays itself out over and over again: now only in her head. "Sometimes in that room I was searching for a rope, anything," she says. But there were no options for an easy death, only a towel and bedsheet. "One old lady gave me a balm, like Vicks, for the wounds."

Siva was studying in Sri Lanka's capital, Colombo, when Central Intelligence picked her up. She is studying again as an asylum seeker in Wolverhampton.

"In 2013, my visa will finish, and I can get nationality in the United Kingdom. And then I will go to Sri Lanka. I will go to Sri Lanka and shoot him [the man who raped me]."

Stage Design and Structure: The folk plays are staged in front of temples. The stage is sited on the centre of the arena selected to be the open-air theatre. It is actually a firm strong circular mound, three foot in height and forty foot in circumference, constructed with either hard earth or sand.[14]

In Tamil areas, *therukkoothu* is the traditional art of public theater, a form of entertainment in villages—often dramatic depictions of kings and deities.[15] In the governing style of the Tigers, as they took control of territories where the cultural practice remained, the content would be more closely curated. Female fighters reported two kinds of therukkoothu in which they often participated. The first was a space for collective grievance, evoking emotional engagement from participants by placing only a symbolic item on center stage. "Wails could often be heard across neighboring villages," one fighter recalled.

The second was the use of music, dance, and dialogue to evoke discussions on contemporary political and social issues—often intimately linked to the suffering of women. Even the presence of women on stage was, in itself, revolutionary. Men would historically play female roles, shaving their beards and mimicking modesty, wearing "long skirts and blouses with extended scarves to match."[16]

It was here, the fighters would often note, that "the average woman could understand how many ways women were not free. They began to make sense of the violence around them."[17] Here all of the violences would come to light: domestic, social, state.

Lighting: Lighting of the stage is done setting alight old cloth soaked in coconut oil and stuffed inside a half coconut. Each half coconut is securely placed on top of banana stumps at uniform height.[18]

Over the years, temples would split under shelling, and the soft sand of public spaces would be collected only under the boots of soldiers.

An entire population would shroud themselves in secrecy to survive, and rape of women would both increase and be pushed into the shadows. In a scolding letter to her brother who left for Canada, written in 1991, a female fighter describes the role of rape in her decision to join the Tigers.

As far as the Army is concerned Tamil women are commodities in the market place: they may at any time become food for the mere lust of those men. Even though these barbaric acts don't seemingly have any impact on people like you, certainly they have had an immense impact on us and inspired liberation feelings in the minds of Tamil women.[19]

In 1961, some fighters remember from their childhood, Tamil women sat, legs crossed, in rows of white saris outside government buildings in Jaffna for days to challenge institutional racism, creating a "festival-like atmosphere, with people singing protest songs and physically blocking state institutions."[20]

In 2018, D'lo, a member of my activist family whose identity hovered between here and there, would bring a comedy staged in Los Angeles to the Eastern shores of the island. A trans Tamil artist, D'lo has pushed his way through every layer of captivity in a fight for his right to exist. Over the years he would tell me, "A really good comedian is in really good touch with our own pain. It is only from that place that art moves society forward." A politics anchored in pain will never be performative.

In the tradition of the therukkoothu, hundreds of aunties who have been protesting in the streets gather that afternoon in a school courtyard to witness "a thinking, politicized being." As she flies in, D'lo's character of "super-auntie" coerces comedic relief. As laughter hesitantly erupts, he moves quickly between time and space offering this collective a way to "inspect your pain and move on, to the next site of struggle." In the narrative of the state the women have themselves to blame for femicide; they are criminalized well before they take to the streets. When I visited in 2015, activists would tell me, "Women will first plead with the state, then they will challenge it." Yes, the law required them to protest peacefully. But, one would note, "I do not believe in the laws in Mexico. They don't protect us, so we don't need to follow them."[21]

Every few years a morbid moment, the brazen killing of Marisela, the rape of a child, will mobilize women visibly, pushing them onto the streets of Mexico. Some have stayed there for the deaths that pile up daily. In the interim they have been plotting. In search of protection from the violence that targets one or more of their identities (women, indigenous). In recognition of the state's calculated failures, they patrol public space armed in Michoacan inside the pack of bike gangs and "autodefensa" groups.

By Valentine's Day of 2020, enraged Mexican women would make their way directly to the Palacio Nacional in Mexico City, armed with fire cans and machetes. This was not the crowd stuck on Independence Avenue in Washington, DC, forcing hope through signs and knitted headwear. These are the women who are "filled with rage"; whose death has been predetermined by the state; who move to manage the discomfort of chronic pain.

A CHORUS

If I share my trauma, it will be put on trial.
My memory will be asked to represent itself under oath.
The prosecution won't rest until they've extracted the wound,
pulled threads to unravel me.
Trauma is a weak defense.

. . . the evidence will have gaps.
Moments of violence will retreat to grey matter.
Revealing itself when I least expect it.
Resisting the invasion of foreign agents;
The therapist, the lawyer, the lover.
Trauma is intentionally elusive.

. . . suddenly, I'll be seen.
In America, embraced by other survivors, provided virtual solace.
In Sri Lanka I could barter it, for a chicken or sewing machine.
It disappears parts of me, as it reveals others.
Reparations rarely heal.
Trauma is a risky currency to trade on.

. . . I'll want it back.
Too late.
The pin pulled detonates reactions that center HIM, and divide us.
In his violence and my confession I have no control.
The story spun will wrap itself around me,
Squeezing.
Trauma hates captivity.

. . . it will be diagnosed.
No Post in a Traumatic life.
When it layers itself,
weighted by the Stress of constant Disorder.
Trauma collapses entire selves into a single moment.

. . . it will be dressed up for donors.
My personal made their political; my violence blended into theirs.
My body of proof evidence of their foes' evil,
because enemy warfare is barbaric and imperial warfare
   humanitarian.
Trauma has no loyalty.

. . . it will ignite a battle of the sexes.
Until the women in power vote for their agenda,
Not my pain.
My minefield of emotions becomes her occupied territory.
Trauma is a turncoat.

. . . it will be trapped.
Bureaucracy waves a wand, grants my trauma three wishes:
end sexual violence, create a task force, a promise from the men
   who rape women.
Trauma cannot make demands of its own.
Trauma is oppressed.

. . . it will be used to distract,
Erecting blinders,
Blocking the view of violent structures
Chased down, it twists and turns,
you won't notice roots of inequality burrowing
Trauma is a tool.

. . . it will be overexposed and underestimated.
Some women are scared they will not be believed.
I fear I'll be believed and it won't matter.
The trouble with trauma is it doesn't end rape.

If it were my trauma I would,

Keep control of where it was placed,
Understand how to organize around it,
Color-coordinate the wheels of justice (slower for some than
    others),
Manage expectations of an unjust system.

. . . position it,
As the logical outcome,
of a society that anchors its political self
in domination and supremacy.
Inside the over-policed neighborhoods,
that valorize and validate violence.

. . . set it,
Against the women's movements,
willing to champion the plight of our gender,
But willfully blind,
to the politics of the deeply dispossessed.

. . . prevent it,
From inviting, inciting more violence,
The expected lashing out
Of a masculinity in collusion
With a fascist state.

. . . feel it,
as a force of radiating destruction
in the cold, calculated protection of a gun,
feel it, eventually, fall behind me,
pushing my political work forward.

. . . and not share it,
Because my trauma, alone,
will not stop this from happening to you, too.

CHAPTER 3

THE STREETS

Target Practice: Guns and Women

> Freedom isn't free, *men say, fingering fresh jangling chains.*
> *The itch, the ache in the crotch as they berate the woman state.*
>
> *By boat, by foot, by tunnel, by air, by will,*
> *by lie, by prayer, by luck:*
> *We have come. We are here by the hand of fate. The woman state*
>
> *Is what we set out from and journey toward, begging knowledge*
> *And grace. Let us welcome—let us praise—the woman state.*
> —TRACY K. SMITH[1]

In America, the mishandling of both guns and women by men does not raise questions of morality. Rather, both reinforce a virile masculinity that fills in the foundation of our society—one whose aggression can justify existence through the biological essentialism ascribed to (offered to?) masculinity. In America, both women and guns are the property of men: a toxic combination whose fumes extend from the chambers of governance to the streets.

It is no surprise, then, that the reality of women picking up guns, of women signaling a capacity for calculated violence, is alarming. Even a hint of women's violent potential will unearth beliefs buried deep in the labyrinth of gender norms and shake a liberal nation's sense of security.

> *By the time humankind reached the stage of written mythology and law, the patriarchate was definitely established: the males were to write the codes. While setting up the machinery of women's oppression, the legislators are afraid of her.*
>
> —SIMONE DE BEAUVOIR[2]

A MAN IN THE MIDDLE

As tightly as America holds onto its guns, it is equally anchored in a self-perception of gender equality as proof of a successful, superior liberal project that secures its stance as a "developed" nation. Both co-construct the core of the American identity.

Among the recent spate of feminist writings on anger and rage, nearly all will pull back before rage finds its way to violence—consciously or unconsciously falling into the flowy folds of the early waves of a feminism that burgeoned inside an antiwar movement, one whose rallying call raised only a two-fingered peace sign.[3]

While encouraging women to resist with (a singular) emotive response to injustice (rage), the form their political action takes in these texts is also prescribed to both stay within the lines of an acceptable mode of resistance (nonviolence) and focus on the agreed-upon target (patriarchy).

Some, like Martha Nussbaum, will question the utility of anger in the struggle for justice, with an appeal to revisit peaceful men (Martin Luther King, Gandhi, and the like) to allow women's anger a pathway to transition into a compassionate hope.[4] Others who insist on centering anger in the struggle, the new "rage feminists," still safeguard their calls to action from the unknown dangers of violence seen only as patriarchy's tool.

In her writing on domestic abuse, feminist thinker Rebecca Solnit writes that "the man framed the situation as one in which his chosen victim had no rights and liberties, while he had the right to control and punish her." While this description contextually fits most cases of intimate partner violence, it is Solnit's extrapolation from his aggression into a broader condemnation of violence that merits further interrogation. "Violence is first of all authoritarian. It begins with this premise: I have the right to control you."[5]

Others, advocating for an emotive trigger to resistance, will often buttress their arguments inside an appeal to a constructive kind of rage, a response to violence that, as Brittney Cooper articulates in *Eloquent Rage*, "help[s] us build the kind of world we want to see."[6] In a similar attempt to constrain rage before it touches violence, Soraya Chemaly, quoting Alicia Garza in *Rage Becomes Her*, cautions of acting on anger: "When it's not used properly, it can quickly become destructive."[7]

In an earlier, more philosophical iteration, Hannah Arendt reveals the deeper history of circumscribing rage: a history that easily lends itself to the kind of gender typecasting mainstream feminists should decry. She cautions "that violence often springs from rage is commonplace and rage can indeed be irrational and pathological."[8]

Solnit herself recognizes the failings of the bigger conversation on violence, writing in 2014 on climate change, "When we talk about violence we almost always talk about violence from below, not above. . . . In every arena, we need to look at industrial-scale and systemic violence, not just the hands-on violence of the less powerful."[9] Yet, alongside most feminist writers, Solnit is unlikely to open her own imagination to embrace the politics (I daresay, the feminism) of violent women.

There is a selective kind of violence that evokes American outrage when it challenges the core tenets of how Americans see themselves. Outrage comes from a fracture in the reflective surface of the society we see around us. A media flash (a mass shooting; the shocking philandering of a film director) is disarming, sparking shock and indignation. Filling out this category of rage is Arendt's reading that "only when our sense of justice is offended do we react with rage, and this reaction by no means necessarily reflects personal injury."[10] The brazen violence of the patriarchy cuts deeply to distort the American view of who we are.

This is the kind of rage that demands, and finds, an immediate outlet. It is in the hastily erected political platform of a reactive tweet. And it lends itself easily to the rapid mobilizing of a women's march. In the outpouring on the streets, each protestor is fueled to sacrifice Saturdays by an outrage at the prospect of a nation where women may not, in fact, be equal to men.

The symbolic power of this type of rage can shift public opinion, create social media celebrities, advocate for better laws, and, on occasion, prosecute an individual perpetrator. Outrage, at its best, gives Americans hope.

In Tamil there is no word for hope. In the earliest incarnations of my activism I tried to locate it, tattoo it on my skin, attach it permanently to myself. I was sure it would be the driving force of my work. Instead, the word handed over to me by my unsuspecting mother was the only one she had available: faith. At the time it felt like a poor woman's hope. But once one decides a tattoo is necessary, the lettering must be inked, even where the meaning remains to be determined.

In her earliest memory, Akila remembers being shocked, then overcome with grief by the death of a neighbor auntie, killed in the shelling. Sandra remembers frustration, indignation. "It wasn't just that I heard of people who were killed. I saw it." Each violation, like markings on the wall of a prison cell, informed an inescapable awareness of their captivity. As their minds and bodies grew into an understanding of the violence around them, they would, slowly, fill with rage.

> Rage can only keep you alive
> for so long. To breathe, I grab onto
> this grail of a noble war that could
> confer honour—and flight, can it
> be?—to my blood. Yes, this is
> my choice, we all need one
> to call our own.
>
> —KARTHIKA NAIR[11]

It was often the virulent masculinity of a racist state that forced a breakthrough. As Thamizhini describes the occupying Indian army soldiers, "when we saw their leers and taunts we felt a frustration, a fury, bubbling over inside of us." This was one of a series of moments, not *the* moment that Egyptian journalist Mona Eltahawy would describe as a "long overdue fuck-this-shit snapping."[12]

To consider the decision to choose violence as a momentary lapse of rationality is to dismiss the expansive reservoirs of trauma that shape the makeup of the women who do. For the women I have known, political consciousness would form slowly as they moved through multiple emotional states to their own political territories. When the violations of the state are intimate, the injury to soft spaces hardens quickly. The female fighter is enraged.

In Tamil, they struggle to find a word for rage. In the summer of 2018, a gathering of young Tamil women activists sought out conversations on how to organize the struggle after losing the war. As I begin my talk, they interrupt me: what is the translation of the word "rage" I keep using?

Having very recently emerged from the constant onslaught of shelling, one young woman is concerned. "Rage, to me, akka, older sister, sounds violent. Isn't it dangerous for women to acknowledge their rage? What if it leads to violence?"

It is a fair question because for Tamil women rage had led to violence—but it need not have. The only way to prevent violence, I argue, is to understand the forces that produced this rage—that pushed women to arm themselves in the fight for self-determination.

Sandra often describes a kind of hope in the struggle, more akin to faith, that is buried deep inside—a faint pulse beating insistently in the din of alarm sirens—inaccessible most days, but keeping her alive.

GUNS AND WOMEN

> *Try to understand this at any rate: if violence began this very evening and if exploitation and oppression had never existed on the earth, perhaps the slogans of nonviolence might end the quarrel. But if the whole regime, even your nonviolent ideas, are conditioned by a thousand-year-old oppression, your passivity serves only to place you in the ranks of the oppressors.*
>
> —JEAN-PAUL SARTRE[13]

Our view of the female fighter has been obstructed by both the moral compulsion to decry violent resistance and a societal drive to divide categories of thought along gendered lines. Where feminist arguments are generally gathered inside sanctioned space for women on bookshelves, the thinking of men on violence is nestled into a political canon.

Among the men allowed to offer political commentary, Mark Boyle, in his dissection of nonviolence in *Drinking Molotov Cocktails with Gandhi*, suggests that "many of us, when asked about our views on violence, vehemently oppose it. It's bad, it's wrong, an aberration of nature that needs to be overcome." He theoretically reinforces Solnit's concern that the condemnation is reserved for cases when "it is inflicted towards those in positions of power (or their interests) and not downwards by them."[14]

Even for those feminists who speak from the margins, activism is cordoned off inside a Western hierarchy of legitimate violence. As bell hooks, who perhaps would disagree with Nussbaum's claim that anger is not essential to challenge injustice, argues in her critique of Beyonce's popular album *Lemonade*, "Contrary to misguided notions of gender equality, women do not and will not seize power and create self-love and self-esteem through violent acts."[15]

From inside the Tigers, activist N. Malathy wonders why "violence on women is extensively reported as needing the attention of the world," with no ability to link this violence to the choices of women combatants.[16]

It is inside the overlapping circles of the moral righteousness of nonviolence and the entrenched beliefs on the inherent nature of women that the female fighter and her motivations are disappeared. If nonviolence is valorized as the only legitimate form of resistance, women are the presumed peaceful, moral core that holds this argument in place. But women in the Tigers and other militant movements did seek a type of power through violence: the power to control the experiences of their everyday existence.

Marcelle Shehwaro, an activist and writer recently exiled from Aleppo, Syria, narrows in on the root of the disconnect: "The real problem is the belief that violence is an ideology in itself," she says, "and one that women are not capable of. It is not an ideology, and women are capable of violence." Over years of chats I have learned that Marcelle's flat affect is not distant but rather an insistence on intimacy: that every word be weighted by her reality.[17]

In some senses, then, Marcelle speaks to Arendt's assertion that "violence is by nature instrumental; like all means it always stands in need of guidance and justification by the ends it pursues."[18]

But for her there is nothing to justify; it need not be in pursuit of anything to be just. She does not feel compelled to break down a binary that never existed on the streets. "If the woman is supposed to be pure, innocent, peaceful," she asks, "what happens when she steps on the street where life is both nonviolent and violent?"

A female protester is hit with a baton—and pushes back. An activist kicks the soldier who threatens rape; a journalist wrestles a gun away from her attacker. These are all familiar women to Marcelle, women who can only be understood in immediate relation to the violence they face. They are women for whom peaceful resistance is a death sentence. The female fighter simply suspends a survival instinct over time.

"You cannot overburden us, Syrian women, all women, with being the peaceful ones."

Patriarchy is enshrined in the state and the society that wraps around it. In a bid to consolidate power, it assumes a hydralike form. The body anchored in the patriarchal desire for domination defends itself with multiple heads: militarization, racism, supremacy.

Where misogyny is the hatred of women, racialized supremacy is the hatred of specific women. How do we understand the women confronted with the fiery breath of one of the heads that seeks to extinguish an entire race, those that choose to fight the enemy that confronts them? The ones fighting not for women's rights, but the right to exist? These women do not ignore patriarchy, but they must first survive to fight it.

Tamil writer Meena Kandasamy posted her thoughts on the incessant violence that both destroyed and birthed the Tamil fighter in Sri Lanka:

> It is impossible for Tamil people to forget the horrors of rape committed by the IPKF [Indian Peace Keeping Force], or the Sri Lanka Army on the bodies of Tamil women, including the female fighters of the LTTE [Tigers]. This is the anger of a people who are traumatized by the memory of the rapes and murders of Krishanthi and Koneshwari, of Isai Priya and Logarani.[19]

Kandasamy fuses Tamil women as private citizens and public combatants, for whom all violence is political.

In *The Seven Necessary Sins for Women and Girls*, Mona Eltahawy suggests that "the wars that female combatants will fight are done so in the name of patriarchy; they promote a violence that only the patriarchal state claims a right to."[20] She is right to point to the patriarchy that is the beating heart of most movements but cannot so easily dismiss the motivations of the women inside them—the women who choose to kill.

FIGHTING WITH MEN

My pen

Is a sharp one

Like

The gun in my hands

But

The gun

Only spits out bullets

My pen

Spews out everything

My poem challenges

Any philosophers

Any learned man

Any Pundit

  —VAANATHI[21]

"I suppose there was a man. There was the leader [of the Tigers], he definitely inspired the movement. He inspired me. But that was the only time I thought of a man." Akila told me this in the aftermath of the war. In her posthumously published autobiography, Thamizhini, captain of the women's unit for the LTTE, offered a similar reflection on the narrow feminist lens applied to the guerrilla struggle:

In those times when the fundamental rights of the average man were denied, their familiarity with oppression became the very reason women were able to endure and develop the inner strength to survive the impact of the crises that faced them. It was as an extension of this, that from the beginning of the struggle they stepped out with courage into the street to enter into armed combat for the liberation of the race.[22]

Priya, who joined Thamizhini's division in 1994, puts it simply in our conversations: "I didn't think much past the need to have all these soldiers out of our village, to live peacefully. After the incident [rape] with Akka, I knew it would happen to me also. Maybe it was to protect me, but I wanted to protect all of us."

Even among those women who join a militancy, the decision to kill is often an afterthought. Whereas the decision to fight demands they unleash a desire to survive violence, the decision to kill requires they sublimate the coherent conscience needed to live peacefully.[23] In the end, choice is captured by the distilled clarity of life on the front lines: the moment, as Akila notes, when morality succumbs to the desire to survive, "the only thought you have is preservation."

From the moment she is taken captive, Thamizhini, once one of the most venerated female captains, is suddenly suspect to the society she fought to protect. Why hadn't she taken the cyanide that hung from her neck in the final days? Was she a traitor?

It was perhaps the unbearable weight of this scrutiny that pushed her to write her own story. I met Thamizhini on one of my earliest trips, when she was at the peak of her power. We stood outside a roadside bookstore on the streets she fought to repatriate, as she pointed to the texts that would further my own political education. "When I was young, we thought Western women had more freedoms, but I think they can learn from our cadres," she told me that day. I was never quite sure whether she saw me as standing closer to her or the West. I would not reconnect with her until years after her detention in an effort to arrange a medical airlift to pull her out of her losing battle to cancer.

Thamizhini, like many of the fighters I have known, gave her life to the struggle. Once it was handed over she could not control how it was used or how it would be remembered. As her own words cover the page it is clear that when she became a figure larger than life, she never intended to cast a shadow over the hundreds of women, foot soldiers, in her command.

When Nedra Rodrigo, a Tamil refugee and scholar-activist, is chosen to translate the text, one Tamil man gruffly tells her, "She should have killed herself." Expectations of sacrifice fall unevenly across the gender divide. After spending years immersed in the captain's words, she responds, "Thamizhini was a woman with the temerity to choose to live."[24]

When I ask Akila if she's read a draft of Thamizhini's as-yet-unpublished memoir, she says she has. Then silence. For a fighter, the habit of discipline has always been intertwined with the pursuit of freedom. Inside the movement Thamizhini would have been the direct commander against whom dissent was forbidden. On the outside there is still a pause before the critique slowly seeps out.

"I agree with some things she says in the book," she begins hesitantly. I wait. "But it was different, you know? I knew her in school. When we met inside the movement, she hadn't really learned to use a gun."

Another pause. "To be a fighter, you must be a cadre, no?"

The year before, I had seen Priya in her home. Priya was in the same battalion as Akila and had been thinking about why her interaction with men was so different inside the movement. "I think because we all had guns." Priya didn't take up arms in pursuit of gender equality, but she remembers it as an unintended consequence of participating in political violence.

"What was to be done with guns, the tasks, they were the same for male and female combatants. We did everything the men did and we never required their assistance in anything." Akila would say often, and in different ways, "We didn't want them involved in our work."

One task stands out for Akila. She had proved her worth on the battlefield and in September 2005 was invited into the Leopard Forces (a team of special commandos) in the armory section. "I remember when we opened each barrel that arrived from Russia." Each weapon was covered in petroleum jelly to protect them. "There was a rocket launcher; I had never held one of those before. Also the M16—those were more lightweight." There were no men there for the task, she recalls. "Even though it was a difficult moment in the struggle, holding each one, wiping it off, I felt powerful."[25]

Thamizhini was conscious of the other fighters' wariness at her inability to wield a weapon in the early days of her work on the political side, noting how when combatants asked which base she was from, the patronizing looks were cutting when she replied that she hadn't had training yet. With a keen analytical eye, she turns her gaze inward on herself and her movement.

> The state of mind of the Tamil woman who wears the camouflage uniform and carries a weapon in her hand is entirely different. The transformation her nature undergoes when she understands that she can protect herself.[26]

In my conversations with Sandra, I often mention the theories floating around in the world about female fighters to get her immediate, expectedly indignant, reaction. She finds even the surprise that women might take up arms a kind of "machista" attitude. I show her the cover of a book that purports to explain the motivations of a female fighter, "Bombshell": a blonde Barbie doll dressed in vaguely ethnic wear, accessorized by a belt of suicide bombs.[27] Sandra rolls her eyes and asks, "These women consider themselves feminists?"

Her first impression in the training camps was that there was no separation on gender—"work was done as a block." She, as most fighters, is not blind to, nor hesitant to, address the presence of patriarchy inside the movement; once the ability to fight one oppression is embraced, all inequality reveals itself easily. "Things are not perfect inside the movement—there are, of course, machista men." The issue, however, was placed inside the tensions of the struggle that could only be revealed and reckoned with in internal conversations.

Like Marcelle, she insists on the kind of nuance the outside view seems to calculatedly crush. "Of course, some men were more thoughtful, and made efforts to understand equality; others didn't." When some men took credit for the work of female cadres, Sandra would fight for visibility. "In the end, the men comrades learn that they have underestimated the capability of women."

In the collective fight for social justice, which Sandra saw as the gender equalizer, she was one of the few women who crossed over into the realm of military commanders, called on to advise the movement in political strategy. As she recounts her role, she sits a bit straighter as if to live up to its import.

She takes mercy on me and sips her tea for a few moments as I scrawl furiously in wider and messier script to keep up, then she summarily states: "Having a gun doesn't make me more or less of a woman."

TARGETING THE STATE

A masculine body is the shadowy silhouette around the target—the measured bullseye in the center. For the female fighter, for most women, the contours of the state are filled with masculinity. They embolden one another as oppression takes shape.

Solnit may be right that, in its essence, violence is about control—but not solely for the domination of men over women. It is embedded in a masculine state apparatus that seeks to establish supremacy over "the others," where militaries enforce the desires of an executive, democratically elected or not. When the state seeks control through violence, the resistance fights for self-determination—for the intrinsic desire to control one's own life—in the same way.

> *It is the particular triumph of society—and its loss—that it is able to convince those people to whom it has given inferior status about the reality of this decree; it has the force and the weapons to translate its dictum into fact.*
>
> —JAMES BALDWIN[28]

In later conversations with Sandra, we are discussing the lifespan of a struggle and the moment when women decide, when the struggle decides, to take up arms against the state. We agree that even framing the choice as a last resort is a luxury; the only reprieve is more likely. Where the rest of the world is concerned with the coercion of combatants, Sandra is fixated on force. "It is the state that forces you, to get the guns, to fight."

How, then, to understand a nation littered with guns, picked up on a whim? Or a populace for whom protection has become an existential claim to identity, supremacy, rather than a bid for survival? As she shifts her gaze to the deep legacy of oppression in America, Sandra reflects, "Black women in the United States, the way I see it, they're very strong and can still do the nonviolent political work. I don't think they are at the moment where they need to take up arms."

This, of course, was not always the case—and may not be to-day. When I broach the subject of women in the Black Panthers with Kimberlé Crenshaw, a comrade of intersectionality fame, she begins as a female fighter would: by reversing the lens from the inside out. "We must contextualize any violence of the resistance in the violence they were resisting."[29]

For most American audiences, the female fighter exists in a land far, far away. To consider female militancy in this country, in our movements, requires a reckoning: the need to see police brutality against Black women as state violence, checkpoints in school cafeterias as militarization, and the death rates from domestic and mass violence as mimicking the figures of a war zone. Each of these realities disrupts self-satisfied notions of America, and all are hinged on the positioning of women denied political power and forbidden violence. In response to an essay I co-authored—a piece highlighting the politics of women who kill their abusers—an editor critiqued the argument as "deeply problematic," claiming it created a "homology between women who take up political violence, such as the Kurdish women of the Peshmerga (PKK), and women who use criminal violence." The real root of his concern, however, is the idea that civilized nations were mentioned alongside the behavior of women in darker nations—"it erases a vital distinction between armed struggle where the state has lost the legitimacy of its monopoly on the use of force, and a vigilante-style revenge attack in a rule-of-law democratic society."[30] In his imagined America, an indiscriminate law will protect women from violence.

As the racial divide in the United States deepens, Black women are increasingly taking up arms. According to data released by the Texas Department of Public Safety, Black women are one of the fastest-growing demographic groups to obtain permits to carry a concealed weapon. Like combatant women elsewhere, these civilian women cite the necessity of carrying a gun—for protection and power. Crenshaw grounds the data in racial realities when she notes that, "the politics of a black woman buying a gun are completely different to the politics of a white woman not feeling safe and buying one." To explore the space between their politics, the violence of civilian women, would be something this particular editor would tell me "risks fetishizing violence for its own sake, normalizing and legitimizing it."

The legitimate use of violence as a form of resistance was as divisive a question in the civil rights era as it is in contemporary conversations on the value of Black life. What has remained clear is that normalizing violence is first and foremost the practice of the state. Groups like Armed Empress and the Black Women's Defense League point out that while women in the Black community feel more compelled to individually take up arms in today's America, historically violence has always been "deeply connected to the black experience"—as collective resistance, according to Armed Empress founder Ty Shaw.[31]

In a public conversation at Yale University, I was asked a question that would become a popular refrain in every lecture I gave: "Do you believe violence is empowering for women?" Before I could respond, a fellow panelist from India quipped, "Well, of course, to hold a gun is to hold power. We all want that, but this is what we have to resist."

I do not agree with the question in the first place.

Sandra doesn't remember always feeling powerful. "The feeling when I held one was not one of pleasure, really. It was of self-preservation, only. There was still a lot of fear in me." Worlds away, she rearticulates Crenshaw's concerns, insisting that one must first consider "the context of the women you speak of. The ones who live in a place where every day you have to look out for your life." She repeated the same sentence to me twice, years apart.

Over the course of a lifetime of violence, there is fear, sadness, anxiety, frustration. A loss of control forms a deep rage that is coherent, calculated. The "rage feminist" will see a violent act as a "snapping" in a specific moment—an individual woman's instinct for self-defense—and some will condemn it as such. The female fighter asks us to expand our view, to see the evolution of a politically oriented consciousness that takes shape through the olio of emotional reactions to violence. It is here that we see violent women as acting inside a process of self-determination: the women for whom resistance is collective. As my coauthor, Asale, and I would eventually respond, "To forge connections between women who resist violence by turning to violence is not a fetishization of the act. It's a reclamation of will."[32] As my own are, Asale's thoughts are shaped in the image of the women she sits with over the years, reflections of women like Racine, who killed their abusers and live, captive, on an island closer to home.

> When I got to court [from Riker's] my lawyer is telling me to show remorse, you know to let the people know how sorry I was. But I didn't feel it. They [her legal team] were trying to frame my actions like I snapped, like suddenly, there I was. But looking back now, I'd say, I didn't act violently because I had enough, of his violence and abuse, not only that, you know, but it was because I knew that I was enough. I deserved my dignity, my humanity. And the police, the restraining order did nothing to uphold what I knew. It was like "By any means necessary," like Malcolm X says you know. That's what I was thinking. How to fight my way back to my humanity because the government wasn't going to give me that, no one was.[33]

For women like Racine acting alone, or as Kimberlé Crenshaw would reflect in our conversations on the women in the Black Panthers, "This quite frankly is the work of defending the community, the work of protection, the work of advancing a sense of self-worth. This is self-determination." As some Americans keep a fierce grip on their right to bear arms, others are fighting for their right to exist.

FANTASIES OF KILLING

It is men, most often, who caution against the exploration of violence in the resistance for fear that violence itself might be fetishized. And it is men, most often, who fetishize the female fighter.

"Violence," singer/artist M.I.A. tells me, of her choice to include guns in her music videos, "is always okay in someone's eyes. In the rap game, and war, it depends on the angle you are shooting."[34]

Maya (M.I.A.'s birth name) is the femme fatale who fits perfectly into the male fantasy of violent women: kohl-rimmed eyes framed by dark hair; perfectly curved figure that takes a fighting stance; manicured not-too-dark-skinned hands grip a gun that extends beyond her svelte frame.

In journalist Dan Baum's essay "Happiness Is a Worn Gun," desire dominates his manipulation of a firearm and fear limits his imagination.

> The sensual pleasure of handling guns is a big part of the habit. Elegantly designed and exquisitely manufactured, they are deeply satisfying to manipulate, even without shooting. Rage wasn't an option, because I had no way of knowing where it would end, and somehow my brain and body sensed that.[35]

I am reminded of an older white woman who approached me after a lecture on female fighters in a Soho public theater. "I thought it was fascinating, but I couldn't identify this feeling. I'm not sure I've ever felt rage like that." Rage and guns inhabit our bodies and imaginations in different ways.

Marcelle would once quip, "I think the PKK is most often the image men see when they think of the female fighter because they think they are cute, pink-cheeked, and fair-skinned." Guns leave calluses on the hands of the female fighter, tough skin forming over the lines of a hard life. In Syria and Sri Lanka, if the rough touch is paired with chopped hair, then she is known to have been a fighter. As one nun in charge of rehabilitation of ex-cadres would tell me, "These ones, the former Tigers, they are undesirable. When their hair grows, it will be easier."

The trappings of femininity are not the militant woman's concern, even as she redefines its possibilities. She takes care in fitting a thick belt over a boxy shirt but ignores the cracked nails and overexposed skin growing tougher as the days pass. As one fighter, Tharani, would write to her brother in 1991 about his notions of beauty, "Our women have shattered such meaningless notions and are demonstrating admirable success on the battlefield."[36]

> The women cadres struggle in the darkness to carry out such routine practices as hair brushing and plaiting. Rifle cleaning was carried out with the benefit of the light of the early dawn. The rifle was a sleeping mate while the holster and uniform were worn like a second skin. Bathing turned into a luxury form of relaxation on odd occasions free from trench digging.
>
> —ADELE[37]

Unconcerned with a superficial loss of the womanhood that made her vulnerable, Akila would note, "When I held the gun, I felt, finally, as if I had some control" over the violence that forged her identity.

———————

In an effort to dismantle the fantasy that stripped her of a right to political consciousness, the authorized documentary of Maya's life reveals a young woman sitting on the floor of a small apartment in Mitcham with a copy of Frantz Fanon's *Wretched of the Earth*. As she crouches over the pages, as if examining contraband, she looks up to the camera and points to the last time the book was checked out—several years before. Recognizing a reflection of her political self, she asks, "Why is nobody reading this?"

> *Have you ever set out in search of a missing half? The piece that isn't shapely, elegant, simple. The half that's ugly, heavy, abrasive. Awkward to the hand. Gritty on the tongue.*
>
> —SHALIJA PATEL[38]

At a bookstore reading once, I was asked if I would consider my work a "pushback" to the status quo. I do not. I have worked inside the institutions that uphold the existing state of affairs enough to know the lines are rigid, unforgiving, incapable of absorbing the impact of thoughtful analysis and unwilling to do so. From years of work with female fighters, I see my work as expanding the political imagination of the resistance. It is here that infinite possibilities inform new political realities, and it is here that the consciousness of the female fighter begins.

For most female fighters with intrinsic motivations to resist, fantasies of political possibilities entered their imaginations in two ways: the women that came before them, and the texts they had access to. In liberation movements across the globe, the political education of fighters was considered an integral part of entry into the movement, but, as Sandra reminds me, "In reality, you were at war, so it was a luxury to read—we so enjoyed it when we could, though."

That same year, emerging from a different jungle captain, Vishaka reflects on her political education. When she enters the secured house we have rented in Northern Sri Lanka in 2018, the younger women activists are filled with a sudden deference to her, a former captain in the movement alongside Thamizhini. Her smile has a sweetness that sets the room at ease. She seems relieved to freely think about a moment in life where liberation seemed possible. "At first, when we heard of the Tigers, we thought only the bad children were the ones who joined."[39] Vishaka was just barely twelve years old, a child, when she learned what a Kfir (an Israeli missile jet known as "Lion Cub") was. Her school was struck in the middle of exams. She would learn the names of her dead classmates much later when she was home waiting for school to restart. "We felt, suddenly, very lost after that."

It was in those weeks that her own akka went to a meeting of the Student Organization of the Liberation Tigers (SOLT). Vishaka was drawn to the possibilities of resistance, but as the next oldest child she felt the weight of caring for her mother and her home. "When she left to join, I looked at my akka whose face I knew so well. She was scared, but I could see, her mind was charged." For Vishaka, her sister's decision planted the seeds of political consciousness, a way to exert some control over the discriminate violence of her childhood.

A scan of Thamizhini's memory is also scattered with dark spots. In high school she spent the afternoon under her desk to avoid shooting by the Indian forces, able to glimpse her beloved principal beaten viciously by state soldiers. After that, she writes,

"Going to school every day was walking on fire." She became the leader of SOLT, chanting slogans like "Student strength is a powerful strength, don't force the hand that raises a pen to raise a gun."

> We were spurred on in the most difficult combat training by the thought that we women of Eelam would one day write stories of courage like the women who joined the battle in the Chinese Red Army, in Palestine and in Telangana.[40]

The mistake, Sandra feels, is to make gender a factor in Colombia, where state violence doesn't discriminate along gender lines. "In our context, in our lives, this was men, women, working together for the same goal. Not to harm people, but to preserve our rights."

Grounding an older adage on the bartering of violence in her own memory of urgent survival, she argues, "In that moment, only the same weapon they use will work against them."

"This wasn't about women or men. The people being targeted had to fight together, right?" Sandra cannot grasp the mental barriers to understanding women's decisions to take up arms. With semi-sarcasm, she asks, "So if a soldier comes at you with a gun, women should respond with what?" she asks rhetorically. "A Bible? A book? Kindness?"

THE BATTLEFIELD

I n society women are positioned without consent. On the battle-field they carefully calculate their own positioning. Akila entered her first battle just before she turned eighteen. "I had joined a queue that I wasn't quite sure what women were lining up for, when I realized it was to join the next battle. I was so adamant that they let me join."

Depending on your position, Akila and other fighters over the years would tell me, the feeling was different as you entered battle. For Akila the first battle was an ambush, the kind of success that was both thrilling and addictive. "On the defensive, it's not the same," she explains. "You are fighting to hold on, so the army doesn't capture the territory, and you can lose."

It is from the defensive stance that enemy strategy has to be anticipated. One cannot move forward in opposition, or scatter in any direction for survival. "Sometimes you feel you are making progress, other times that you are just being diverted, and redirected."

We are sitting today in a tea factory that Akila started with other ex-combatants, harvesting leaves unique to the jungles of former Tiger territory that she knew intimately. It is 2019. She apologizes every time the phone rings with jarring interjections. "No, we speak English and Tamil." "We are on eBay and Amazon, you can order in the UK, yes."

When she returns to the conversation she begins to sketch out lines on the table. "When you are in the front lines, you are the most prepared. It is high risk, but you could also make real gains in territory." It is, of course, she explains, not an actual line. It dips and jags in response to enemy movements. The Tigers were also insistent about the language they used for positioning, anchoring themselves linguistically in the Global South, in Tamil territory. "We do not use British names, like Alpha, Charlie. We knew the points announced over the walkie-talkies as things like 'Sarangani,' 'Serai.'"

The second line would be a little farther back, a few hundred meters. "From this place you are still fighting, perhaps gathering information, or even the occasional direct skirmish." In this place there was more waiting, more time and space, for camaraderies to develop between the women not constantly on alert.

Akila never considered being pushed back to the third line of defense a defeat. The territory might be lost, but it had not been lost yet. "But also, when you are here, this is when you have to be creative to win the fight, isn't it?" Akila wants me to consider not just the participation of the female fighter, but her contribution in so many different ways. "We didn't just participate, but were a part of everything, at every point in the struggle."

Sandra was high enough in the hierarchy to be a part of the decision to advance or retreat, though she acknowledges that many women were not. She seems to struggle with life off the front lines more than Akila. Perhaps it is the pressure of the pretense that the FARC has not yet lost: she is still fighting, but it's not always clear where she is meant to aim. Still inside the momentum of life on the battlefield, she remarks, "We, the FARC, have to move forward, but perhaps in a new formation now."

The position of the female fighter is constantly shifting: the lines of defense they draw, breaking through the concentric circles of culture, community, and state repression holding every marginalized woman captive. How she negotiates a policy world that negates her politics in the interest of peace, reconciles the outward performance of motherhood and marriage with the demands of an internal political identity, and navigates new political terrain as it shifts beneath her—the decisions of the women who seek recognition of their right to self-determination.

CHAPTER 4

A PANEL: THE THIRD LINE

The Missing Politics of Peace

> *We were asked to move back to the third line of defense, not when it was a defeat, but we were no longer in a position of power.*
>
> —AKILA[1]

A panel is a flat component, typically rectangular, that forms, or sets into, a wall. Another kind of panel, another kind of flatness, is a collection of experts in a straight line, thrice removed and untethered by ties to the suffering of others. The line is taut and cannot absorb tension, only reinforce existing frames. The object of their concern is often the women from "developing" nations and the terror-prone men that oppress them: "a secondary population vis-à-vis the 'occidental' majority, an estate prone to disorder that needs to be controlled," as Sergio González Rodríguez says in *The Femicide Machine*.[2]

I have often been asked to fall in line with colleagues in these consensus-building endeavors, in the shadow of the Capitol

Building. I am always immediately conscious of where I sit, cordoned off inside the earth's northwest quadrant of power.

> Translineal spaces alter the meaning and representation of identity and function. Each side of the border exchanges information and then modifies itself in relation to the other: the two sides clash, dialogue, repel and fuse, either temporarily or permanently.[3]
>
> —SERGIO GONZÁLEZ RODRIGUEZ

Where the white women seek seating inside masculine spaces of power, I am a placeholder for diversity inside a world divided by its commitment to (some) feminist ideals. If the subject is the plight of refugees in a humanitarian crisis, audience members have teared up assuming that my life has mirrored that of the women who are languishing in camps. If the subject is security studies and the women who join militant struggles, my arguments are placed in the margins—notes, or anecdotes, to consider peripherally in the more noble pursuit of peace. In both development and peace building they cannot concede to the entirety of my arguments without uncomfortably turning on themselves, but they cannot deny the argument's right to exist for fear of dismantling a façade of progressive politics.

Of the current feminist waves that crashed inside a gulf of conscious thinkers, only the very first iteration, white feminism, penetrated the world of foreign intervention (both charitable and military). The lives of female fighters like Akila or Sandra, nestled inside the feminism of a third-world liberatory project, reveal hidden agendas while presenting a direct challenge to the global safeguards erected to protect political power consolidated in certain states. Though far from a war zone, it is an important space for fighters to hold the line against the misguided intrusions of a policy panel.

> *How do you lay out a narrative of oppression*
> *without succumbing to the pornography of pain?*
>
> —SONIA[4]

When I meet Priya again, in 2010, she is no longer in the austere and organized space of a training camp—she squats in the sands of chaos, a refugee now.

She has been squatting for some time. The position is not as comfortable as it used to be. In the jungle they would hold their muscles tight, silencing bodies poised for attack. She sweeps her sari out of the way as she starts to cook the day's rice. "This," she says, as she pours the water ration that just barely rinses her equally meager rationed pile of rice, "this is what they have given me." She jerks her head in the direction of the dusty open space. Her two small children are breathless, covered in dust. I realize she isn't referring to the pot in front of her. Two chickens run between their legs, inducing squeals from both sides.

Priya knows she was raped by a soldier, but the medical evidence does not exist. She is a widow, but his death certificate does not exist. His photo, her proof of life, is conceptual at best. Perhaps he is one of the "disappeared": a category without a cause. She is an ex-combatant, but she has only kept a tattered patch of her uniform as confirmation. She hands it to me so they cannot attach it to her. As they moved from the last stand into barbed wire internment, she slips into the catchall category of a postconflict "war victim."

In her first days in the camp Priya had watched with the others as a large charity group from the West gave the women who were raped three chickens. They were meant to return with cages. The first chicken died the next day. "It is hard to keep chickens alive in the jungle," she tells me. She gets up slowly, moving toward the children. She walks in pain, lifting one foot higher than the other, the folds of fabric lifting ever so slightly to reveal the plastic appliance that imperfectly mimics an appendage. She surveys the two remaining chickens. "I cannot even run after these things," she says, pulling the children away. "I suppose now that I am handicapped that kind of thing [rape] may not happen again."

In the camps there are rumors of a desk, established in each camp by the United Nations High Commissioner for Refugees (UNHCR) where an officer sitting on one side would document the sexual violence reported on the other. Only once did a woman report actually seeing the fabled desk, flanked on both sides by government soldiers.

When we sit she forces the fake limb to bend beneath her. She calls me Thangachi, younger sister, and tells me, "I will rebuild my life. But I am afraid. If the soldier sees the chicken, he will know I told them I was raped. What if he decides to reveal that I am a fighter?"

"I am not at peace."

On your simulacrum of a desk every lock. Motionless, waiting. Stowing blades and extermination lists. A line of names. A sequence of letters burning the papers. This place is hot and disguises itself as oxygen.[5]

—DOLORES DORANTES

In their condemnation of violence in the resistance, Western feminists are quick to point out alternatives. In particular, the transfer system they are most invested in: empowerment programming.

Elsewhere, I have argued with colleagues that much of the contemporary empowerment conversation is narrowly centered on the sexualized condition of women in the developing world (rape, prostitution, trafficking).[6] This singular focus at best detracts from and at worst overshadows the larger forces of political subordination that perpetuate all forms of violence against women.

The authors of the original empowerment approach, activists and scholars from the Global South, sought to mobilize the political consciousness of the oppressed through three core components: power, conscientization, and agency. As the term entered policy jargon, each of these has been both subverted and repurposed. Power has been exchanged for livelihoods, political education on oppressive structures for skills training, and agency reduced to a choice between raising chickens or cows.

This approach serves two purposes that both reinforce Western feminist worldviews and re-entrench inequality. The first casts the intervention into the lives of third-world women as a moral imperative, and any critique to be an attack on the inherent "goodness" of the intervenor's intent rather than the interrogation of a skewed system. Second, the victim, sexualized in an extension of a feminism hyperfocused on sexual liberation, will not be viewed as a political actor.

In colonial times, the *Englishwoman's Review* created a repository for knowledge on the "natives." Here, Indian woman prey to the evils of local cultures are noted as "special and deserving objects of feminist concern." It is a sentiment that settled deeply into the foundation of contemporary humanitarian pro-gramming, even if its officers are careful to publicly decry any remnants of the "savior" in their practice.

> *Nobody in the world, nobody in history, has ever gotten their freedom by appealing to the moral sense of the people who were oppressing them.*
>
> —ASSATA SHAKUR[7]

The violent female fighter, and her uncomfortable position-ing in the aid complex, more clearly reveals the process of depo-liticizing: she is neither fully a victim to be saved nor a political agent to be supported.

Moreover, she reveals a disconnect so expansive as to border on the absurd. Combatants who once hoped to be chosen for battle, now missing legs, are offered a pastry cart; snipers who once cut their own hair off offered beauty salon training; the cap-tain who recaptured a key crossing point, Elephant Pass, offered a sewing machine.

A scholar, as Ann Carson describes it, "is someone who takes a position. From which position certain lines become visible."[8] I am looking for the lines that connect the ex-combatants who hide in the shadows, now permanently positioned in the rear guard. I transcribe the ex-combatant testimonials, compiled over several years of returning to Sri Lanka after the end of the war, that won't be featured in the marketing pamphlets of charities:

> "When they gave us sewing machines, we ex-combatants were in no condition to do any kind of work, let alone sew."

> "You can't earn an income. This, sewing, the government is just doing this to say that we are reintegrated into society."

"We are told a seamstress is a fitting job for girls."

"Even to move around, to go to a job, to express their opinion, all of the ex-combatants are filled with fear."

"The priest told me to just be patient, and stitch. I didn't want to. I used to just watch them stitch."

"They told me to try and get some goats, or chickens, or cows from an NGO so I can start my life again."

"I have lost sensation in my hand, so I often cannot feel the needle."

"This is the only option we have been given. So we have to sew."

To reveal the racial underpinnings of a feminism that misunderstands the lives of the marginalized will be met with, at worst, public denial and, at best, unsolicited advice, relayed through private correspondence to me, the fighters, Marcelle, on how best to stay inside the lines.

Development agencies and white women might take exception with being dispensed with that quickly—and you might lose them for further action.[9]

You sense in different ways that you are always being accused. I am not a terrorist.

—MARCELLE[10]

In my experience, anger is narrated in either staccato statements or a steady stream of consciousness. Marcelle's both flows rapidly and is punctuated with sudden twists and turns constantly threatening to throw you off. She is, now, globally positioned to map an analytical trench through the rubble of Aleppo.

On that particularly frigid evening in New York, both our noses hurt. She has a cold, and a surgeon has just operated on my defective sinuses. I am nursing a broken heart, and she is, tentatively, in love.

She moves between the facts of her experience and the fiction spun around her.

In this moment, Marcelle sits between herself and the projection of herself. She is keenly aware of the image each audience demands. The image is retouched, carefully cropped to fit each political agenda. She is Syrian and speaks English perfected in "white institutions," her mother was killed, she has been abducted, but she never took up arms. She still supports, and criticizes, the armed resistance.

When people first meet her, she says, "I am in nobody's picture." She examines the parts of herself left on the cutting room floor. From Sutangazi, Turkey, she looks down at herself in Aleppo, Syria, certain of only two things: as a priest's daughter, she was meant to be a virgin; and she was a journalist. Each a distinctive threat to her existence, both combined to form a hardened, protective, political perspective.

She was no different than any other journalist whose intimate knowledge of violence embedded deep political sympathies. The state demanded these sympathies for the Syrian soldiers. "But it was them, the army, who threatened my life. Not ISIS." Preying on perceptions of piety, rape was meant to silence her. "We are going to rape you, in front of your family," said the secular soldier.

It is perhaps more useful to think of drivers to violent extremism in terms of an absence of good governance.[11]

Sex, for Marcelle, was liberating in its tie to survival. Inside the sudden simplicity of life in a war zone, "you eat, find shelter, and have sex." She doesn't remember the moment when she herself became a part of the conflict, but she remembers when she understood she was not safe alone. In that time of visceral insecurity, she recalls, you can only be "safe in the tribe." Sex tied the tribe together.

It wasn't long after the conflict touched her that Western arms extended their support. Unable to afford the false modesty of Western women, she tells me, "I am a very well-known activist."

The projection of her on NGO whiteboards and butcher paper is the cinematic version of a story for which she did not release the rights. She is asked to tell it so many times she sets it on repeat. Westerners struggle to locate the bad guy as she edits her memories to fit the funding. For donors, she knows "we have to be suffering."

When she attends the World Humanitarian Summit for Syria in Istanbul, she notices something—the care with which everyone's clothes cling to their shapes. Everyone and everything is tailored. She looks at me as she searches for the word. "It all feels . . . bourgeois."

As with most such convenings, during the day political powers point to their own interests on moderated panels, leaving evenings free for them to present performances of their emotional investment.

> *Compare those societies that respect women and those that don't.*
> *If you think about societies that empower women and protect*
> *women in vulnerable situations, those societies . . . don't harbor*
> *terrorists or pirates. . . . Therefore it's in our national interest. . . .*
> *There's a one-to-one correspondence. Don't tell me there's no*
> *relationship between national security and the empowerment*
> *of women.*
>
> —AMBASSADOR DON STEINBERG[12]

UN women are the ones who focus on peace. "They don't care about politics, they only need peace," Marcelle notes. Syrian women, she feels, are not interested in their offer of global sisterhood, in all of its simplifying sameness. Syrian women are pro–Al-Nusra Front, pro-regime, pro-revolution, and, sometimes, they change their minds. Whether she is in Turkey, Geneva, or Beirut, she sees the same thing. "They want to bring women in from all sides, to love each other."

> Most cultures—be it in the developing or the developed
> world—have been defined by elite men. And most cultures are
> mechanisms by which to reproduce structures of repression
> and exploitation, including gender inequalities. This provides an
> argument for a global sisterhood![13]

Indicators, at the United Nations, are generally used to measure the success of the United Nations. For women in the Global South, the numbers cannot capture the entirety of their repression nor the necessary ingenuity that drives their political work.

When outside actors try to understand the role of women in political life, they are often confused. A specific identity targeted by state violence will be disappeared inside anodyne categories for minority populations.

> Please remove any reference to the term "identity" in your report, 'Political Voice and Barriers to Participation in Asia.' Please replace with 'marker.'[14]

One of the indicators used to gauge women's leadership and political voice in a country is the number of women CEOs. As Marcelle meets with her would-be saviors, they steer her toward their own focus—women-led NGOs.

These Syrian women are figureheads operating under a Western female CEO. They implement programs designed elsewhere, creating fast products within six months. Indicators meant to measure social change, Marcelle discovered, are "measured by everyone saying they are happy." Suffering is exported and exhibited—handicrafts for the soul.

> What if we brought some of these poor girls who are being trafficked here, like to New Jersey? Then they could live a normal high school life, you know, go to prom and things.[15]

Marcelle insists on participating in political negotiations, refusing to sit in the chair reserved for women predestined to be peaceful. The tipping point for each foreign government's interest keeps shifting—every few weeks they defer to someone else's pain. Each time, she explains the violence of her world to a new low-level officer, and each time, the ladder-climbing individual within a bureaucratized institution reads her their scripted (apolitical) approach. She reflects back on this space, these conversations: "I suppose, for the 'local' activist, the goal is to tailor suffering."

In the evening she watches a play, a reenactment of children dancing before being bombed in Aleppo. After the final scene, the dead Western children get up to accept their applause and walk off stage. Marcelle shakes her head. "I feel like I am in a circus."

As she moves back into herself, away from her shadows on the screen, we discuss depression. The kind you live with and learn to laugh through. The kind that stems from a darkness that demands its right to your life. The kind that is heavily weighted in reality.

Marcelle herself was abducted by the Islamists in Aleppo. She herself watched her mother get shot at a checkpoint. She herself faced ISIS. Some people call her a hero, others a terrorist.

In the language games the powerful play with the powerless, terror is the definition of a threat that is given, radical is the description of resistance taken away. She doesn't know how to live with the labels. It is only when her anger stands in the way of her own projection that the image is constructively obscured.

She pauses to sip her tea in the rather bland chair bought hastily to fill the corners of my empty apartment. She checks her phone, looking for the flash of his affection. I am inwardly grateful for no notifications of his anger, for the dimmed screen that is only reflective.

Earlier that day, she had presented to a donor foundation in New York. She tells me, "I answer how my mother died like it's the daily news. While I am eating pizza." They ask her, now, what happened in Aleppo.

Her laugh is dark, but not defeated, as she repeats the question to herself. "What happened is, the world left us alone when we were dying—and by the world I mean the West—and now they want to tell us how to live."

———

As it slipped through political agendas, the uninterrogated brand of white feminism that defines development became the foundation for the recently coined "feminist foreign policy," a worldview cushioned in Western analysis meant to alleviate the suffering of women in the developing world. It is here that what scholar-activist Lila Al-bugod calls the "securo-feminist" was born, and takes up the offensive position.

> In your critique of whiteness, do be careful not to fall in the reverse trap whereby actions of people are first and foremost defined by their race or position.[16]

Any challenge that emerges from the actual chaos of conflict-ridden lives is met with linear thinking that carefully angles around accountability or acknowledgment of historically entrenched structures of inequality—skipping straight to "If this is a problem, what is the solution? What are the recommendations?"

One particular panel steeped in conservative thought would still satisfy the diversity requirements to escape overexposure and public scorn. "The Future of Women in Extremism" featured four women, one (me) of whom was of color: not a manel, but not inclusive. The chosen title is a nod to a burgeoning cottage industry inside the world of security studies. As one feminist foreign policy pundit would publicly proclaim, "The pool of young extremist men is no longer our only concern." Feminist concern now extends to embrace the perceived plight of the female fighter.

> *You will at first think I am painting the lines myself; it's not so. I merely know where to stand to see the lines that are there. And the mysterious thing, it is a very mysterious thing, is how these lines do paint themselves. Before there were any edges or angles or virtue—who was there to ask questions?*
>
> —ANN CARSON[17]

Over time I have learned that very few of the people seated behind a policy panel have spent time with a female fighter, or any woman who has taken up arms, and that we have all heard the same words on different panels, at different times. They have analyzed the colors of her Tumblr feed, viewed her patterns of behavior distorted through social media, read the work of colleagues who have not met her either.

They will not give up their positioning to meet in the fields of violence; they will only issue a polite invitation to join them at the table. From a safe distance they are absolved of responsibility for the forces that radicalized her.

When the hostilities ceased in Colombia, Sandra too was offered the opportunity to do nails, or makeup. When she asked about college, the international organizations who descended on the newly minted "post-conflict nation" asked how many sewing machines the ex-fighters would want.

"They don't offer things we need, like legal support, only beauty supplies. At one meeting there was a short-term project for ex-fighters from an international group called 'Brooms and Mops for Reintegration.'"

> Speaker 1:[18] We have found that most women leave militant movements because they miss their "creature comforts." Like having a glass of wine with your favorite sitcom.

The first time I meet her, Sandra's "comunidad base," the community from her military base, is gathered inside a dilapidated motel-like space, "Hotel Casa Americana" in central Bogotá. The peace talks have been going on for almost seven months, as the nearly thirty men and women ex-combatants in the home live in limbo, waiting to learn of their fate.

At first, Sandra is wary but welcoming. We meet at 6 p.m. most days, after everyone has returned from the state-mandated lessons they all attend. The release of pent-up tension is palpable as the group enters and the sterile space fills with banter and easy conversation. "The course they have developed for us, is, of course, about peace—how to be peaceful," Sandra explains with discernable scorn. Inside Casa Americana, they are drafting and redrafting letters, to "sue the state" for violations during the war, and to express their political demands.

Here, too, in the reeducation of the female fighter, women are told that they are inherently peaceful. "I cannot understand this perspective. What has affected you, in your life, that is what makes you who you are. Has the violence of the state not affected women?"

> Speaker 2: We have found that many women are drawn to social media accounts of militants by the bright colors and photos and Arabic men on horses with long flowing hair.

We talk about moving between spaces, from home to camps, from the front line to this new positioning on the periphery of state-sponsored peace talks. "You have the same ideology, the same politics, but in each space they understand it differently, you know?" she says, a sentiment that I see myself in. Sandra continues, "And then each of these distinctive spaces—they are also shaping your politics as they happen."

The next time I meet Sandra, the government has kicked them out of the hotel. "We were criticizing the 'projects' they offered to us. Never mind, we don't want to be taken care of." In the sparse office space above a crowded empanada bakery gifted by the Norwegians, Sandra is now operating under the FUCEPAZ (Colombian Foundation of Ex-combatants and Peace Promoters).

She speaks with a steady steeliness, betrayed by the occasional smile. "Nimmi, do you think we have given up too much in the peace talks? Have we been taken advantage of?" I don't know how to answer. I do know that movements that never compromise meet a sudden death—that the FARC narrowly escaped the fate of the Tigers. One year in, Sandra, like many other female cadres, has no interest in exchanging her politics for false promises of power. She will not be pulled to the table. "I will do what I have to for the peace process, but I will never be demobilized." It is a declaration I have heard many times before.

Speaker 3: I agree that among other things we must consider the challenges of good governance third-world nations face.

I never blame good governance, only state violence. State violence is a central motivation for female fighters. As the talks begin for the FARC, they split along expected lines and state violence is almost immediately disappeared. It is decided that the Gender

Subcommission will hold separate talks, adjunct to the political peace talks in Cuba. A young researcher would explain to me, "While women were an integral part of the movement, somehow the conversation has become the demands of the collective versus the demands of women."

On the political side they would discuss militarization of agricultural land (managed by a largely female peasantry), indigenous people's rights (indigenous women had marched across the country to demand a recognition of their community's existence), a diversity of local leadership (women who sought political office would do so at the risk of femicide), a new economic model (based on programs designed by Sandra herself).

As the silos formed internally, reinforced by international practices around "women's issues," Sandra would be invited to panels hosted by the Women's Ministry inside Foreign Affairs and UN Women, asked only to discuss sexual violence. "In this way," she says, "they would discredit the FARC, but also the political demands of our women political combatants."

I tell her of my work to dismantle the false promise of empowerment; she asks that any writing be translated into Spanish for the FARC. "I fear, Nimmi, that in all of this, sewing machines and peace talks, our combatants are losing their politics."

The next time we speak, Sandra is losing patience. "There have been a series of failures in the peace talks." She cancels our meeting in Bogotá the first and second time. She has to be in the lowlands for emergency work.

She apologizes when we eventually speak: "When you give your life to a political project, your life is not your own." She tells me some women have been demobilized and are back home. She pauses. She answers the questions she perhaps knows by now I am about to ask, but she speaks carefully, deliberately. "I cannot guarantee that nobody is going back to war; they would have a million reasons to do so."

"Women," she reminds me, "are not born pacifists."

Thamizhini recalls a feeling of relief when Bala (chief strategist of the Tigers) and his wife Adele landed via air taxi from the Maldives to participate in peace talks. Seeing the leader "laugh and talk in a relaxed manner filled everyone's heart with peace, and confidence."[19]

As the talks began the government would insist they begin with "civilian needs," and the Tigers would demand a decision on political rights. As in Colombia, Syria, everywhere deemed "post-conflict," the NGOs entered—carrying with them the illusion of progress toward peace.

> Speaker 4: We need to make women in these societies "pro-social." They can be key to preventing terrorism and promoting peace.

Allowing her memoir a momentary indulgence in irritation, Thamizhini writes, "Even hearing the titles of their [international NGOs] little projects, like 'Rebuilding Peace' and 'Creating Harmony Between Ethnic Groups' and so on became unbearably annoying for the Tigers."[20]

In the talks, decades before the FARC put down their arms in Colombia, the movement suddenly split along gender lines under the weight of international pressure. Thamizhini would represent Tamil women in the "adjunct meetings," a subcommission on gender, while the political issues would be discussed by the male leadership. "I didn't really have much faith that the women's meeting would actually accomplish much," she notes.

"Yet it was an unusual experience for me to have the chance to speak openly with women from other societies."

They were tasked with discussing domestic violence and economic livelihoods for widows. They did not discuss the experiences with a public war that seeped into the private space of homes, the shells that killed husbands, or the white vans that disappeared them. They did not discuss why women joined the militancy.

Speaker 5: Women joining these movements is often simply a question of who they bump into. Either on the streets or online, they can be easily recruited.

Behind desks erected by the international community in the capital, Colombo, I would hear some of the ongoing talks being discussed. The breakdown in women's meetings over the urgency of issues would spawn an analysis of its own: "The Tiger women are not really interested in peace." As Akila remembers that time, "No, we were in a political fight. We are trained to fight for that space from the state. The other issues will be dealt with internally."

The ten-year mark of the end of the war has just passed, and Akila and I are sitting at her own desk, in her tea factory. She considers the parameters of peace, or living peacefully: "There is no more bloodshed. No dead bodies. No shelling."

In the years immediately following her capture, she was unsatisfied with work that wasn't political. She couldn't find work in her village, as she moved with the mark of one who has been detained. She ran for political office inside the Tamil opposition party, but when she earned over ten thousand votes, she found she first had to face off internally—with male politicians, the traditional keepers of party politics. "I disagreed with their idea of nation building; coming from the jungle it made no sense to make concessions to the state. Some of these men didn't even fight, to know what peace should look like."

Eventually she would lose interest in the sterility of this kind of politics. As we speak she is interrupted by a barrage of phone calls—the ring moving between two handheld phones and one landline. "Yes, we can ship to the UK, even Nigeria." "Yes, the tea is ayurvedic, very calming."

She has hired fifteen other ex-combatants who cannot find work to help manage her budding tea business. She feels the movement gave her the desire to work to support Tamil people, and the confidence to carry it out. Every Sunday Akila visits the army camp nearby, to register her activities with the occupying military force.

When the noise stops for a moment, the same words come out in a different order. "Yes, now there is no shelling, no dead bodies, no bloodshed. But if you do not feel free . . . is that peace?"

CHAPTER 5

THE SECOND LINE

Manipulations of Marriage and Motherhood

A kila wasn't the first woman to sketch the lines she lives inside in my notebook. Over the years women in Sri Lanka, Colombia, Mexico, and elsewhere would position themselves inside the shapes that left them open to attack and the ones inside which they would take cover. The state was often too close—uncomfortably, intimately close.

> See, here, Nimmi, this is where the camp starts, and my tent is here [she draws a square]. There is the barbed wire we cannot cross [line]. There, right next to the wire fence is the bathing area [circle]. The army camp [she pauses, to draw] is just here. Right here [she draws a square, touching the line].[1]

I would spend years documenting this violence: the destructive hands of the state on women they held captive. This was not unique to Sri Lanka. As countries entered into an uneasy peace and state forces became more visible, professionalized, to outside observers, new narratives would quickly spin around these same violated women, separating the state from culpability. As a Sri Lankan army lieutenant would explain to me:

> You see, Professor, from the outside you have understood this wrong. This, the violence women are facing are from inside their communities itself, it is a problem of Tamil culture. We hear of a lot of alcoholism and abuse. Our military guys are very disciplined, so they are not involved.[2]

I would hear some version of this from NGOs in Tunisia (the problem of Muslim culture), white feminists directing peace talks in Colombia (machismo culture), and the police force in Atlanta (Black culture). At moments I have sensed a nearly audible collective sigh of relief at having identified the problem, the perpetrator that both bears the entirety of the burden of violence and releases all of the forces around it of responsibility: culture.

To highlight the "barbarism" of local culture has always served the interests of the oppressor over the desires of the oppressed. In policy conversations on the participation of women in violent movements, Western analysts are quick to bring up the repressive cultures of developing countries as a motivation for the female fighter or, worse, read her decision to join a militancy as simply an extension of a "culture" rooted in self-sacrifice.

The implicit definition most intervenors operate on is a culture that is static, fixed through time and space—a set of customs attached to a native community. This definition does not consider that in the disrupted lives of women living through violence, culture will wrap itself around context—a force that is both restrictive and protective. Nor does it consider the cultures imported by interveners, cultures of dependency, militarization, and others that quickly settle into a way of being in the everyday of local lives.

Working closely with local researchers in Afghanistan, a nation whose culture has been entirely constructed for external viewers through a gendered lens, one village close to the border found that young girls had suddenly stopped going to school. One father told me, "Since the military arrived, there has been an increase in military checkpoints on the road to the children's school." A "cultural" explanation was quickly dismantled as the accused went on to explain, "We heard of a sexual assault as a young girl passed, so if we cannot walk with our girls some days, we don't send them."[3]

On the inside, a woman from Afghanistan (or Colombia, Mexico, or Sri Lanka) is incessantly, relentlessly aware of the culture that can, at times, dictate her every movement. It is a minefield that both combatant and civilian are forever navigating. Not unlike violence, when it comes to culture, she is backed into a binary for the sake of the outside world: to either condone or condemn her own culture.

The villages under Tiger control were uncharted gender territory still laden with seeming contradictions. I would encounter a female fighter questioning a young woman not wearing a long skirt or chastising her for not riding a bike the correct way. In the eyes of the combatant, there is unquestionable clarity: "What else are we fighting for, then, if not to protect our culture?"

In the aftermath of the war, in an open schoolyard in Eastern Sri Lanka, an exhibit is being put together. A tree molded of papier-mâché stands in the center. A woman is painted across the spread of the trunk, a rope across her chest. Around the tree hangs an artistic rendering of mortar shells suspended in mid-air. Students are asked to walk around the tree.[4]

It is a rendering of a real-life incident: a local woman whose family had given her 4,000 rupees to hold as she fled the shelling. When her husband demanded the money, she refused. In his anger, he tied her to a tree, sealing her fate under the shower of shelling.

The woman, an artist and activist, asks students who walk around the tree, "Which is worse for Tamil women? This violence of a husband or the state?" Women will always contest the binds of culture on the inside.

A longtime Tamil activist on sexual violence defines the circular lines she lives by:

> I will explain it to you like this, Nimmi. I follow the 3–6–9 rule. I can only directly support the woman three feet from me. I can only hope that she impacts the family six feet from me, and the community nine feet from me.[5]

This is how she manages expectations of social change; the levers of state power are out of her reach. Culture will graft itself onto the lived realities of war zones, holding the line around a community under siege. Women are the pressure point in the interior, absorbing the force of the offensive. Here, the pain is intense and the cries are muffled. A younger Tamil woman activist in Toronto remarks, "If you say anything, you get pushed outside of the community, outside the circle—the only protection you have."

INNER CIRCLE: MARRIAGE AND MOTHERHOOD

I was betrothed, but unmarried, when I reached the checkpoint into Tiger-controlled territory. The women fighters inside the roadside huts were at ease, secure in their current position. They handed us, my not-quite-husband and I, the small yellow form for a visa. We marked "married" for a single visa (the cheaper option over two individual passes) and handed it back over with the required rupees.

The rigid faces of the fatigued women fell into gentle laughter, Tamil flying rapid-fire across to neighboring huts as the amusement spread. It was only after we settled in a Jaffna hostel that a tiny mirror revealed that the Tigers were, in fact, laughing at us. I was wearing a black pottu.

Being married was my entry point into the Tamil community back home and the newly independent state cordoned off from the outside world by the cultural markers of Tamil-ness. But a married Tamil woman is marked: by a red dot, not a black one, just above her eyebrows, in the middle of her forehead.

In the Cosi coffee shop, Akila says she didn't think of it at the time, but as she grew into her role as a combatant she saw the movement as an escape from marriage.

"I understand the concept of getting married, but when I see Tamil women I wonder, why are you behaving like a slave to your husband?" She considers the role of marriage in her own motivation to join, and moves from the inside out. "Women fight against many things, at once." Holding her captive in the inner circle is marriage and motherhood, while just outside the home hovers a judgmental sociocultural stratosphere, itself encircled by the rigid force of the state.

My dear brother, you have questioned as to what a woman could achieve. We are the products of a society which confined the women folks to a small circle saying that they are weak and frail and can only perform selected jobs.

—THARANI[6]

In a Brahminised Hindu wedding ceremony, the bride will make the circles around her with decorated feet: stepping carefully as she lifts the heavy sari pleats to walk around a purifying fire pledging love, fidelity, respect, and trust. The bride does not speak.

Decades after the first female fighters joined the movement, Adele Auntie would recount to me the animated discussions that took place in households with four generations of women. Here, "with the first fighters, inside a hundred years of community history,"[7] the concerns of women would be openly discussed, including abolishing cultural practices like dowry that had held women as property of men.

MOVEMENT

Vishaka was married in 2001, on the inside. In 2001, Tamil communities fell inside the Eelam's (Tigers' state) administrative lines. Marriage laws for cadres had been well established by then.

> Among most ranks, love and marriage took place easily. When members fell in love, they had to inform the chief secretariat through their respective commanders. The marriageable age for men was 29, and for women 23. It was expected that at least one of the two had to have served for at least five years in the movement.[8]

Vishaka remembers the age being twenty-one, but she had reason to rush: "Theyvan and I were "very much in love." Both were battlefield surgeons who had learned to improvise and treat the wounded with ingenuity and minimal tools.

Vishaka laughs when she remembers the event, of deep cultural significance, slotted into the demands of her political work. "I had a surgery at 4 p.m., I was still working on a stuck piece of a shrapnel, and the wedding was set to be at 7 p.m."

She remembers at least a hundred people crowded inside the makeshift wedding hall. She has come to give me her wedding video, transferred from a VHS tape to a flash drive to me, to transport off the island.

It takes a few different apps to open this content. Images twist and slide in the film, the kind of flashiness austere Tamils allow themselves only in capturing momentous cultural ceremonies or family portraits. Vishaka's slight frame is overwhelmed by the thick vermillion silk of her sari, her face adorned only with eyeliner and a red pottu, thin strands of white flowers falling over a messy plait.

The footage is grainy but some details are clear. There are no circles. The bride and groom are seated next to each other behind a desk, across from an official from the Tiger Marriage Secretariat. She stands and speaks, repeating the words of an officiating female fighter. There is an acknowledgment of ancestry, place, a knowing acceptance of the man beside her as her "life support," and an intent to live jointly inside the freedom of an independent state.

In still shots juxtaposed in cinematic overlay, Vishaka's cohort of bare-faced combatants flank the groom and bride, in oversized shirts and baggy pants cinched with a belt. They are without even earrings, "the universal adornment of Tamil women," as N. Malathy puts it.[9] It was a decision the first batch of fighters made themselves, that jewelry would hinder the fighter's performance. Looking straight into the camera, the women stand at attention but smile easily inside this happy reprieve.

SOCIETY: CAUGHT IN THE MIDDLE

In one of the moments when we meet over the years, Sandra marks the time since we've last seen each other: "Estás gordita."

My usual translator, a local Colombian activist, is away at the time and sends her roommate. The young man turns to me and offers his bland, American translation: "She says: You've gotten fat."

I protest. It's the shirt, maybe? She smiles and shakes her head firmly. She is stating a fact. Unhelpfully, the translator repeats, "She says you have gotten fat." I sigh. I explain that I have gotten divorced recently and have taken to sublimating emotional angst with breakfast sausage and chocolate coffees. Sandra is pleased. "Ah. That is good. It is much easier to do political work when you are alone."

Valeria, one of the women close enough to wrap themselves around me in moments of emotional crises later reassured me, "No, in Spanish it is also used to describe someone looking healthy, beautiful." I didn't entirely believe her, but my wounded vanity took refuge in Sandra's outlook on my political potential.

"Women sometimes seem to me to either want to fight all men or marry them. In the movement the men are just our allies." Sandra's own distinctive brand of guerrilla feminism emerges organically as a young man, an ex-combatant, anxiously interrupts to softly ask Sandra if she might sign some papers. It is winter in Bogotá, and Sandra is dressed in a fitted red blazer over a soft pink sweater, with bright pink lipstick. Sandra is not married; she often says it doesn't interest her.

In the early years of my research, around 2006, I spent time in the Eritrean capital of Asmara speaking to female fighters who were members of the Eritrean People's Liberation Front (now ruling the country). At the Eritrean Women's Development office, an older woman would advise me, "You can tell the former fighters usually because they will be the ones wearing high heels, nails done, hair done—even early in the morning."[10]

I wonder if the external glints of gold, glitter, or soft pinks are Sandra's own assimilation into a disarming femininity or simply the desire to be desired.

"When we reentered society, it was a sudden loss of self. It feels like society is not suitable for us." Vishaka, like others, tried to identify the source of the stigma to be shed, though she always came away unclear. As a surgeon, she occupied the higher echelon of cadres in the movement. Now, she laments that "we have dropped to such a low level in society"—a status she feels in everyday interactions and attributes to any number of reasons after the demise of the movement. "Perhaps my gender, caste, fear of association, anger at the movement . . . or all of these things."

> *I had once stated that it was only through participating in armed*
> *conflict that women could bring about change in society. And yet,*
> *I couldn't say that along with armed combat there was a parallel*
> *program undertaken to bring about societal change.*
>
> —THAMIZHINI[11]

In 2008, the year before the final onslaught, fighters had begun to slowly come out from the movement into territories recaptured by the state. Sitting with young folks applying for university, one young man brings up the movement, and his sister's role.

"My sister is quiet, but not afraid of anything. She was a combatant for seven years. I am proud of her for fighting." As he speaks of her, a few other young Tamil men nod, seeing in his sister the women they have let go, or lost, to the struggle. I note that it is not often that I have heard such thoughtfulness from

Tamil men. He begins again, emphatically articulating his feminist credentials: "In our family we tell people we have a woman
who fought for the Tamils. I think men and women are equal."
He is happy that his sister is married now with two children. And
you, I ask? "Me, I'm not married." He pauses. "But I would not
marry a fighter."

In the years that followed, in conversations across the former
Tiger-held territories, female fighters would try to shed their former selves to assimilate, unnoticed, into Tamil society. Tucked
inside marriage and motherhood, they might be spared social
scorn and escape the surveillance of the state. If neither was an
option they often turned to the church.

One church property is walled off on the western coast. The
sisters have been informed ahead of time and allow me to enter.
Through the meticulous gardens, rows of ex-combatants are set
up inside one large shed. Their heads are bowed above cutouts
of delicate white lace. They look up out of curiosity, then quickly
back down as the Father arrives and describes the scene:

> You see, Nimmi, they are stitching wedding gloves we will send
> to Colombo and abroad. They have strong arms from their
> training, and discipline too. The gloves are very popular be-
> cause they are intricate, and they sell very well for brides.[12]

Hands clasped behind his back, he is equal parts headmaster
and deity as he glides in white robes through the silence. I do not
want to ask any questions, but he looks sternly at one woman.
"She has questions for you! Speak up, child."

She looks up at me. "We are very happy working here." The
Father moves on, satisfied.

In other rooms, in other spaces, the whispers of the nuns are
those I have heard reverberate across the island:

"She will stay in the convent until she loses the weight from the baby. She won't want anyone to know about the rape, or she won't get married."

"She is staying here until the scar heals, and her hair grows long again. Then her mother can propose marriage."

"She has learned to make careful designs in icing for wedding cakes. This is a skill she can use if she can't get married."

I have met one of the fighters before, and she sits with me as the other girls sweep the yard. Her eyes would once squint to gauge the projectile of a bullet. Now she rubs them, trying to soothe the ache after hours of meeting the precision of a needle's eye. "I cannot even speak freely. But why did so many of us join? We were slaves and didn't want to live as slaves. We wanted to live free. And now . . ."

Sandra mentions her time in detention a few times and only in passing. She remembers being offered two things on the inside: food and beauty products. "This was supposed to help us to feel normal again." Mostly, she felt useless, swallowed by the interminable empty time. Sometimes she reminds me, herself, "I was there. I was in jail."

She contextualizes her own suffering in the collective: "Nobody will talk about the women who have been accused as war criminals, nearly fifty of them, separated away from everybody's view." If the female terrorist is not considered human enough for rights, I could only imagine the torture reserved for those with an even darker designation.

Of her time on the inside, Vishaka mentions a few human rights groups stopping by to "check lights and fans," the open washroom, the food occasionally slipped to those in solitary confinement dismissed as "psych cases." Sandra's statement is short: "Like animals, that's how they saw us, that's how they treated us."

Vishaka was allowed to move around the confined space, when needed, to treat patients. It was on one of these visits that she saw Thamizhini. Only her two eyes were visible through the netted mesh; the rest of her disappeared in the state's captivity. She whispers, "You are a godsend. Please tell the Tamil people, outside, that I, too, am prisoner. I did not sell out. I am still with the movement."

> *Have you felt constricted by the spaces of your body— eyes,*
> *hands, fingernails, ribcage, limbs, skill;*
> *dwelling-rooms, floor, ceiling, windows, latches, doorknobs—*
> *condemned to a fixity?*
> *And by the space of a clock; enclosing the repetitive movement*
> *Of the second-hand, minute-hand, the hour-hand;*
> *Such that the rhythms of the body and architecture of dwelling*
> *aid the*
> *regulation and incarceration of bodies, space, and time?*
> —UZMA FALAK[13]

Thamizhini, Vishaka, and Sandra would enter into a society smugly satisfied with new evidence that women should not, indeed, be involved in politics. A cultural community will always be both dagger and shield to the women it births. Sandra came out to look for allies and found "a lot of the women I fought alongside were only interested in homemaking" (aided and abetted, of course, by the sudden influx of conciliatory sewing machines) as they slowly shed their political (public) identities.

On the outside, Sandra felt that society had suddenly changed. "When you have seen so many things, how can you look at anything the same?" It was in Cuba that she would find her comrades. Outside the media glare of the peace talks, Sandra meets with female fighters from Guatemala, El Salvador, and Ireland.

Always insistent on distinctive contextual realities, here Sandra notes that "in some ways we all went through the same things, similar histories of oppression. I was really glad to have the opportunity to learn from them." I inwardly lament that the complete destruction of the movement, and with it many international ties, would prevent ex-Tiger women from attending such gatherings.

Both Sandra and Akila mention that they are expected to marry, if not have children. Vishaka shakes her head at this kind of thinking. "Even if you try and get people to think, to motivate women politically, people will call you crazy. In this society, there's no space even to think."

THE STATE: CIRCLES OF CAPTIVITY

At the beginning of the war, a Tiger would never be taken captive. When they sensed they were trapped, they would bite the cyanide pill that hung around every militant's neck. A fighter from the early batch of female trainees would report of the first female martyred fighter:

> We were in our bunkers firing at the army. Hundreds of Indian troops had jumped out of their vehicles and were firing as they moved towards us. Mortar shells were exploding everywhere. We knew the army was advancing quickly.[14]

At the end of the war, marriage was the final line of defense. Auspicious or semi-auspicious figures were asked to bless the hurried arranged marriages inside refugee camps, by remaining parents, aunties, and elders desperate to keep their girls from recruitment into the movement's last stand or from the soldiers quickly infiltrating safe zones. Marriage was the last layer of protection.

Anuk Arudprasagam's searing fictional depiction, *The Story of a Brief Marriage*, is a tale that lives inside a singular moment on the battlefields. Dinesh, a young Tamil man caught in the shelling, is hastily engaged through relatives to a young Tamil woman working in the clinic, and considers his fate:

> Who was there to arrange a marriage for him now? The fact was that soon he would die, and he could spend his last few days with a person, with not just a person, but with a girl, a woman, a wife. He would be able to make her feel secure and she would be able to do the same for him also. Perhaps they could do the same too, before they died.[15]

In 2014, a British documentary team released a compilation of documentary footage containing images blocked from the view of the world. In one of the final scenes of *No Fire Zone*, the bed of a pickup truck is loaded up with young fighters, men and women, surrounded by military commanders. All of the female fighters have very short hair; some have covered their heads with baseball caps. Several cry silently. One young fighter, short hair tied up, is still pleading with the army. Dressed in a long nightie, with the gold *thali* (wedding necklace) and earrings, she looks out at the laughing military men.

With no arms, no UN, no journalists, and no strength, as Latha would say, "What do you have left in you to fight back, if there is not even food inside of you?" When the soldiers came the aunties would have tried to protect the young woman, likely with all they had left: marriage. When the young woman looks back from the cargo bed, the powder of a fresh red pottu is still falling around the frame of her desperate face as the truck drives away.

Of the many concentric circles that capture the female fighter, the largest in diameter and reach is the state. It can touch her, yet she never gets to hold it accountable.

MOTHERHOOD

My amma doesn't talk about the violence that occupied the periphery of the first half of her life often. She mentions, in passing, that when there were riots, when tensions were high, she would wipe the pottu off her forehead before leaving the house to walk to medical school. That was how they knew you were Tamil. She was marked. Whether a pottu, a hijab, or a hoodie, the state asks besieged communities to sacrifice identity for security.

Sandra feels "women are seen as useful in society only in their role as mothers." I am relatively certain Sandra does not have children, though she does not discuss family to protect them from the risks of her political work. Akila recalls her sister saying with disdain, "You should settle down and be a mother; enough with political things."

Some fighters were mothers. In the early days of the movement, the Tigers, the FARC, and many other structured insurgencies would begin to open childcare centers where fighters would leave their children sometimes for weeks at a time. Farther north on the globe, at the same time (the late 1970s), the women's movement in Venice Beach, California, would come out with publications like "Momma," "catalyzed by the new woman's consciousness to recognize the needs of divorced, widowed, separated and never married mothers who are raising children alone," and forming collectives to care for children while women left for political work.[16]

I often remember the years after the war, the moments when women like Janani had told me, "I have my children to think of now, but I would fight again." When Sandra asks why I don't stay longer in Colombia, I explain that I have a son to return to. She smiles. "So bring him, leave him with us. Leave him with the FARC. We'll take care of him."

When my son was nine months old, he traveled to Sri Lanka. He was half as old as the cessation of hostilities, and I was there to investigate crimes committed as the Tiger state fell to government forces.

It wasn't an easy task. Those affiliated with nongovernmental organizations were banned from high-security zones. Journalists were almost immediately abducted. Government critics were forcefully silenced in the din of victory parades. Information came at a high price. And, I was a Tamil.

I was a lot of things, actually: a scholar, a human rights researcher, a writer. Perhaps most viscerally in the year that my body tried to reconstitute itself from predestined trauma, a mother.

The sensitive cases, the weighted bellies that bore the burden of proof for mass rapes, were sent to the church. Military men lined the edges of the church courtyard; I wouldn't be able to walk in.

Various guises to hide my identity were discussed: don a nun's habit and pretend to be studying in the church; accompany a medical doctor; drop off baby bottles as a charitable donor. In the end, it was decided that the soldiers should see me carrying my son.

With my son in my arms, I was suddenly soft. I was viewed as a mother—to be fleetingly separated from my actual, political self was the safest choice.

———

Many of the fighters I have known, particularly those with children, have fled the country after the war. Women from Eritrea, Sri Lanka, Colombia, El Salvador, and elsewhere often crossed each other's countries en route to the fabled freedom of the West. At borders, checkpoints, and detention centers, they would gather, "the mothers," waiting to plead their case. I am brought in as an expert witness, to confirm if their fear of home is credible.

One case would begin at 5 a.m. New York time. Even over Skype the hostility of the white-wigged judge in the British lower courts is palpable. Half dressed, and half awake, I have just begun to discuss the defendant's political life when he cuts me off.

"That issue is separate," he snaps. "We are discussing whether her life is at risk as a single mother." This particular case was to determine the risk of return for "female-headed households," mothers living alone in the military-heavy war zones in Sri Lanka.

The judge continues, with increasing animosity, "Can you confirm that the defendant was not affiliated with the Tigers?" When a social movement emerges from an oppressed community, everyone is affiliated. The details were different, but the case was always the same: the Native Woman vs. the Colonizer—the precedent having been set well before either the defendant or I were born.

In any asylum case, you must first establish the peaceful nature of the defendant—that she is not a threat to the host country. Then, gruesome evidence verifies the violence that makes her a victim. Finally, you must prove that the violence is recurring and poses a threat to her life.

If she is a mother, the first task is infinitely easier. Mother-hood as a construct transcends borders, party lines, and cultural differences. For juries and activists alike, the aggrieved mother is a deeply emotive cry to rally around a pure (not political) cause.

Revealing his desire to deport, the judge pushes further: "After the peace, isn't life much better for women?" No. Not for the women who fought for a cause, the women who supported it, the women who lost.

I argue her innocence in the intractable conflict. I use data to determine the likelihood of rape by the military. I manipulate emotions with her motherhood. I select the negatives that might attract a positive determination.

Once they believe she is docile, sexualized, and morally sound, she is allowed to stay.

"If you are one of those mothers, you will be killed." The scholar I am sitting with inside a sprawling Mexico City bookstore is not speaking of women who have taken up arms, but those who are publicly mourning the death of their daughters. "These mothers are anti-state, for femicide, yes, but also corruption, negligence, violence."[17] The daughters are marked for existing—bodies thrown aside, skin covered with cuts and teeth-shaped indents—and the mothers for protesting.

The mothers of Mexico, Sri Lanka, and elsewhere would draw much of their inspiration from the Mothers of the Plaza de Mayo in Argentina, heads covered in white scarves stitched with the names of the children taken by the state in 1977. Eventually the group would split between those who would accept some government concessions and the mothers (branded as "radi-cal") who saw an opportunity under the banner of a politicized motherhood to pursue the political work of preserving life through a direct challenge to a fascist regime.

Leela, one of the "Mothers of the Disappeared" in Sri Lanka, cites the women of Argentina as an inspiration, women they hope to meet. We stand just inside a blue tarpaulin tent softened by the gauzy saris running alongside it, where Tamil mothers, ammas, sit on two makeshift wooden plank stages. Today would be their last of five hundred days of protest at this site. My son has just turned eight years old, and he wanders between them, my phone hanging perilously from his fingers, asking to take a picture.

Some have fallen asleep in the shade cast across the wooden planks. They have gotten used to repurposing saris for cover since their land was taken by the military. Waiting through the stillness of midday heat is familiar too from their months in internment camps.

My amma, visiting the homeland from the United States, asks, "Will you accept the money the government is planning to give?" She had read in the local papers that reparations were the latest political platitude offered for their pain. Leela looks at me, then back at my mother. The response is sharp: "Will you take money for her, your child?"

My son comes over to sit on my lap: he has taken photos of their photos. Each mother has gone through their printed photographs to choose their favorite of the child they once knew. It is laminated, and then wrapped in a plastic bag: they are willing to use them, but they must be protected.

Their children did not disappear. They are detained, or dead. Mexican writer Roberto González Villarreal says, "Disappearance . . . is a specific repressive technology—an assemblage of actions, omissions, confusions, in which many agents participate."[18] Life, for the mothers, is framed in terms of death. Leela says, "I only want to see my son before I die." I visit her home—a kitschy mausoleum of sorts—built around her son's material remains. She caresses the brand-new sneakers he never wore.

A pained face turns earnest: "You know, Nimmi, I have a very strong mind! I wanted to study politics; I could have, if not for the war." She pauses. "My mind is very strong," she repeats, reinforcing the sentiment to herself.

Leela joined the Tigers to fight for the rights of her people. In the collective of mothers, some of the women were combatants in the Tigers, and some were combatants in other rebel groups. Motherhood is simply a means to an end. "If we organize as mothers, people have more sympathy," Leela explains. In the hands of women acutely aware of the cultural commodity they wield, it is a tool, sharpened to eke out the political space they have been denied. In Mexico, the Madres Buscadoras' appeal for their loved ones was met by government agents handing them shovels—to dig for answers.

They are focused, Leela says, on diplomats from Europe. "Why would we fall at the feet of the perpetrator to ask for our children back? We choose, instead, to fall at the feet of the witnesses. The ones who watched it happen."

CHAPTER 6

THE FRONT LINES

Reclaiming Territory

TERRITORY

The female fighter learns the cycles of life inside the biosphere she moves through. She will trek through mud, altering ecosystems with her footprint. Commands from higher up will not help her navigate; she needs signs in the moment that the enemy is encroaching: the crushed branches, the sound of an approaching kfir, the white residue of phosphorus smoke that burned through the barrier of flesh and leaves alike. With every step some organism is still alive, others dead.

The female fighter's instinct is to protect the territory that is rightfully hers. Sandra watches the land she defended slip away beneath her. "Instead of thirty-one zones in FARC control, now there are twenty-six," she laments, when we spoke in 2019. "It feels as though we lose territory every five agreements."

Territory is precious.

Sandra's question lingers. *Did we sacrifice too much?* She reminds me, "The members of the FARC are still incarcerated. I was, no, I *am* incarcerated. To speak about politics is now illegal. We are not free."

Akila, too, views postwar political life with a similar cynicism: "I cannot speak publicly very well, but I believe you have to be trained to be a freedom fighter." Wake up before dawn. Duties. Political studies. Field training. "Even a small luxury, sleeping in, will make you weak on the battlefield." Akila is clear on who can be considered a fighter. "To be a part of a movement you must sacrifice."

When marginalized peoples are left to fight over the scraps the state leaves behind, lines in the sand are instinctively drawn for self-preservation over solidarity: in grounded realities and metaphorical battles for political space. In the contemporary moment, some in the women's rights movement are policing the boundaries of biologically gendered bodies, while racial justice movements grapple with divisions between the oppressed that worked American soil and those fleeing oppression elsewhere in search of free land. Across struggles activists cling to territories demarcated by specific traumas, not the collective pain of state violence. Resistance is parsed into smaller and smaller boxes of belonging. Territory is contested.

LAND

By the time I felt comfortable calling her "Auntie," Adele was making me *paruppu* (lentils) in her home outside of London. Today I have come to understand the process of guerrilla political education, as it emanated outward from the epicenter in the jungle. Her frame sinks inward, as it does when she speaks of her late husband whose iconic image looks down on us from every wall. "We would find each other, and they would come. The Eritreans, Palestinians, Sudanese freedom fighters. Everyone would sit on the floor of one small room in East London and Bala would lecture."[1] Malathi's reminder rings true: the struggle happens in many places, in many different ways. She would not be the only one to describe this room as family. An ex-Tiger would tell me of that time, "We would have done anything for each other." As the image formed of these impossibly cool revolutionaries gathered in hippie attire to strategize violence, I thought of the current fractured political landscape where individualism was so often confused with identity. There must have been disagreements between these activists back then. How did they all so organically, so intimately, find common ground?

In 2017, a former Tiger on the Eastern shores of Sri Lanka was the centrifugal force around which the people gathered to demand their lands back from military occupation. I had come on the last day of the month when the government had publicly promised to release all the privately owned lands blocked in a high-security zone.

Dressed in a tightly wrapped sari, Malathi still stands at attention. A fighter embodies the line she defends. As we speak, she barks commands, an unbecoming act in the political imaginary of philosophers like Hannah Arendt. She pauses to tell me, "Some people want to gather in town. I think, why should we take the protest to the streets farther away? We should sit here, on our land, until it is released."[2]

Loitering in faded green military T-shirts and sweats, the soldiers are comfortably in command of the village. Some sneer and snicker as they open the gates to a small portion of occupied territory. Oblivious to their presence, the villagers begin running as if to get in before the path to their homeland closes again.

As I walk behind the villagers, a nearly adolescent boy made little by malnutrition demands to know my name. He insists on English. He offers me his, before he reaches down and grabs a handful of soil. "Tamil. Eelam. You know it, Nimmi?" I nod. We stop in the dirt he remembers to be his own.

Without a notebook to document descriptive insight, like Akila, his aunt is moving around the empty space drawing lines in the dirt with her finger. "This is where we had farmland. This is where my brother's house was. This tree was planted by my grandmother." A former Tiger herself, she is conducting a visual survey to note the missing plots of home: the land still behind razor wire.

The boy is unconcerned; he grabs the ground again. After years of displacement and disorientation, today his grin is wide-toothed inside a tiny mouth. As the soil slips between his fingers, he chooses from the available English words with care. "I . . . am . . . very happy . . . today."

Every community under siege has a time line seared into their collective memory, tracking, as one Kashmiri poet puts it, "the razor-wired passage of time." For Tamils, May 2009 was the deepest cut, for some, marking the end of time.

In pursuit of scorched earth, and with the blessing of regional superpowers, the government of Sri Lanka brazenly committed war crimes in plain sight: the hospitals where Vishaka sutured patients were shelled, nearly half of Latha's village was massacred, and Thamizhini was one of the remaining Tiger leadership not summarily executed. Tamils have used the darkest terms to try to draw global attention to the bloodshed on those beaches, landing on genocide.

With distance from the frenzied days when I, when we all, tried to amplify the screams on the island in our appeals to the West, I fear that as a wounded collective we fell prey to the false formula well established for the victimized woman: an expectation that laying bare our trauma would move others to act. We believed that revealing the stain set into our souls would create political change. It did not. *What happened is, the world left us alone when we were dying—and by the world I mean the West.* Marcelle's apt words would capture the experience of the Tamil community years before they would be realized in Syria.

Civilians that survived would be caged, with no rights or mobility, inside internment camps. Cadres like Akila were forced into known detention centers, the less fortunate, hidden torture cells. Tamil land would eventually resettle under military occupation, divided into plates on divergent paths.

Years later, on the eve of my son's ninth birthday and the tenth anniversary of the last day of the war in Sri Lanka (the day the leader of the Tigers was killed), the resistance is gathered in a new formation. In Canada, Tamils from here and there fill out the auditorium space in front of a scattered half circle of activists, artists, and scholars ready to present. This is not a panel to explain or analyze pain. Queer, trans, indigenous, and cis folks are at the forefront of this reckoning inside a fallen struggle's radiating circles of impact.

An indigenous scholar, Sylvia Saysewahum, speaks first. "Our bones are protruding from the graves in land that is occupied." She first acknowledges the rightful ownership of the land on which she stands. "I am not an activist, I am not an environmentalist. Those are my lands. I am fighting the occupier's terrorism."

The summer before, some of us in attendance had walked together on the beaches of the final massacre in Sri Lanka lost in grotesque wonderings on whether the sudden patch of greenery in a military encampment sprang from a mass grave. We knew then that any movement amongst the living must be tethered to the bodies at the root of this grass. *We must move forward in a new formation*, Sandra said, often to herself.

Tamils know that even after the cessation of hostilities occupied land is always unsettled.

―――

The contours of my own connection to the homeland are layered: my positioning superimposed on the map of my parents' memories.

This generational land that will never be inherited has attached itself to me after nearly two decades of listening, organizing, rebuilding with the women who force my thinking outside the lines. On the outside, this work has formed a protective placenta, warding off stares, sustaining my life inside a space only mine by birthright. It is military-occupied but cannot be controlled.

Inside, the land has settled in me like a contentious marriage. The middle part, when romanticized notions fall away and you realize that you will not find some authentic self here: when you allow the sharp edges of the disorientation themselves to redirect you.

Over the years I began to chase intertwined histories: the legacies of our land and my people. Addicted to the lure of political possibility, I needed more information: more boxes.

A tiny childhood box with a precious photo of family, a fighter; a shoebox of poorly photocopied testimonies of torture framed by blackened edges; a tattered white box that once held reams of blank paper filled with disintegrating printed proof of a revolution. Inside these nested boxes lies the answer to why women choose violence. Adele's question returns: *is it really complex?*

In the tapestry of diasporic American lives, someone mentions someone else and we follow a text chain upstate, through a small colonial-styled town, always landing in the warmth of a suburban home erected in exile.

On one such evening, foyer-hovering small talk is omitted at the sight of aging books stacked beside a tower of boxes with faded markings on each side. I am hungrily scanning the scrawled labeling for a clue of which fragments of the female fighter might lie inside.

Uncle wants to mix us a favorite cocktail while we, three dear friends, begin the hunt. The conversation is stilted—curiosity splits my attention between our host's living reflections recounted from the kitchen and the writings of long-dead revolutionaries lying across his study. As nearly discarded memorabilia filtered in to fill in my rented living space, these diaspora homes felt as if they were built around them.

My comrade hands me a book, open to a black-and-white image: "Look, your pata." I tell our host of the lineage that tied me to the man and ask if he happened to know my grandmother, the question pulling me closer into conversation with him.

He returns and hands me the carefully garnished, perfectly sunset-pink Negroni and nods. "I knew Devi well. My mother would join her to canvass for Tamil politicians. It was when she was canvassing that my amma was killed by an army shell." We fall silent as the two rooms collapse into each other and Uncle's shoulders turn inward. Loss can make you concave.

I do not take anything home.

When we leave that night the car fills with only the soft thud of drops hovering between water and sleet. I cherish my time with this Tamil family bound by our ties to the struggle. Sometimes the intensity of debate descends too quickly into an emotional sinkhole as trauma pushes its way back up, until one among us finds the humor to puncture the pressure.

A few miles into the heavy silence, a crack in consciousness. The one who only knew war as a child reflects, "I think all these older people are trying to reconcile many things. But perhaps most of all they struggle with the idea that their contribution to the struggle will never be acknowledged now that the Tigers are gone."

TERRITORY

At moments when the battle for emotional clarity raged inside me, D'lo gently advised that consciousness grows "when you crack the skin and let the soul come out."[3] D'lo grew beside me in forced childhood community gatherings and chosen adult families. He has defied all the attempts to delineate. The pain, he promises, is both necessary and temporary. It is the core of the deep work to find the connective tissue that binds us all in struggle.

Part of his process is an intentional blurring—the quick jump of a body on stage, between spaces. "I think there is a myth created out here [in the West]. Refugees are thriving. Resilient. They bounce back."

When we travel together back to the island to be in conversation with local activists, he absorbs the pain of female ex-combatants. "Our people are fatigued. This is not resilience, this is some basic-ass survival shit. Resilience comes from some available space to be held in their pain. That isn't here."

In between these conversations we sit on hostel beds, once as I nurse a dog-bitten toe trying to placate the phobias it triggered. He laughs at me, and I lose interest in my injury as we try to map the place of the female fighter in the complex terrain of gender.

"If gender is a spectrum in between the poles of a binary, then the female Tigers I have met are closer to the transgender or nonbinary than they are to cis folks."

The lines he sees are not visible to many others. "Trans folks in America and female ex-combatants are living under the radar, living under attack." Both, he feels, leave their house not knowing if they will come back. In the United States, he hears new conversations, in Black, queer organizing spaces, on how to protect fragile lives—some dabbling in the idea of violence.

Earlier that day, D'lo performed for hundreds of aunties and ex-combatants in an overheated classroom on the Eastern shores of the island. In a true testament to his comedic skill, he elicits laughter across a cultural-linguistic divide.

"Lightness is important. Comedy reminds us that the dark shit isn't so dark that it's gonna kill you."

D'lo pauses often to make sure his audience is coming with him as he advances—as he does with me, that night. "The question is, Nimmi, if our people aren't gonna be free on their land anytime soon, how do we create the space for them to feel free?"

RECALIBRATE

Akila knew her role in the struggle. "I was a good sniper. I could quickly recalibrate a gun, to make sure it hit the target."[4]

To calibrate, she explains to the civilian, is to hone a weapon to measure the range of a projectile. I later learn the word itself is linked to the French *calibre* ("degree of importance") and the Arabic *qalib* (a mold for making bullets). In America it is a word some children were forced to learn in classrooms before they could read.

In the clarity of the battlefield, in lives lived on the edge of death, the target is clear. Off the battlefield, the view is more occluded. Sandra's refrain is on replay for herself and many others who are left with only the battered landscape of our political imaginations. *Move forward.* She falls back on navigational instincts: "We must use the updated information available to us to determine which fight is important."

When I began my research inside the white walls of the academy, my target was the scientists who dissected political life to discover a rebellious man whom they viewed with anthropological curiosity and pity, never considering the role of violent women. As ancestral knowledge, narratives, observations, and testimonials replaced the selective texts of a biased discipline, I began to recalibrate.

I no longer want to prove that women rebel too. I want to reveal the ways in which women facing the barrel of the state's gun absorb the impact, recoiling before they resist. These women did not offer up their trauma for others to pull into their agendas but held their pain inside their own fight for political change.

Sandra and I often discuss how to strategize toward a collective struggle. "A part of my training as a fighter was also research. It was in these allocated hours that I read about the Tigers, noted what we, in the FARC, could learn from them."[5]

To find our own place in the struggle we must look across the horizon of the Global South, and deeper into tales only our lands know. We must see, in their entirety, women like Hua Mulan in fifth-century China, said to have released her foot bindings (a coveted feature of the feminine) to blend into a male-dominated army ("Our women have shattered meaningless notions of beauty," said Tharani); Lady Trieu in third-century Vietnam, who entered folklore as the nine-foot-tall rebel against Chinese occupation, declaring, "Why should I imitate others, bow my head, stoop over and be a slave?" ("I will not be a slave to the state, or my husband," said Akila); the Apache warriors on our own occupied lands, like Lozen, who crossed the Rio Grande with her rifle high above her head to beat back the imperialist ambitions of both the American and Mexican armies on indigenous land ("I wanted to be brave like her too," said Vishaka).

> *After the encounter at the Akwa check-point he simply could not sneer at the girls again, nor at the talk of revolution, for he had seen it in action.*
>
> —CHINUA ACHEBE, *Girls at War*[6]

The raw narratives of moments of violence and vulnerability that shaped the women at war, the women chronicled here, disrupt dismissive constructions of female victimhood and force a new reckoning of the relationship of violence to political power in the pursuit of social justice.

These fighters, and the ones whose legacies persist, repopulate learned histories with new female figures—ones that do not seek idolization, only recognition. They offer new territories for women to be complex, constantly changing, conflicted, political actors while fighting to expand our collective political imagination of resistance. Each one provides a magnetic pull on the compass of our consciousness as we map out new cartographies of struggle. As Akila reminds us, in the unconventional warfare of the oppressed, the front line is high risk, but it is only here that one *suddenly feels like anything is possible.*

> *It became easier to bear our situation when armed with the knowledge that in a place not far away, Tamil girls just shot the fuck out of anyone who snatched their rights. It was thrilling to lust after the smoking-hot Che Guevara in his beret and his stubble; equally thrilling to lust after these incredibly brave women.*
>
> —MEENA KANDASAMY[7]

Sandra calls just days before this text is finalized. She is wondering how we are coping in the pandemic. When I ask the same her voice fills with anxiety. The FARC, she says, are dying. She pauses and clarifies the enemy.

"Not the virus, Nimmi. Not dying, sorry. Killed. My comrades are again being killed by the state."

ACKNOWLEDGMENTS

Writing my way into this book was my weapon. I broke through circles of captivity to rebuild a new life sustained by the support of so many.

To Meena, Fanta, Rupa, Fathima, Thulasi, Kate, Carinne, Nicole, Sheriden, D'lo, Katie, Shobi: You occupy territory inside of me—constantly moving from heart to head. Listening and laughing to pull me out of darkness. Debating, reading, and thinking with me towards a reimagined existence. I carry each of you with me. I am grateful always for you, Valeria: my constant comrade in intertwined internal lives of curiosity, children, and crises.

To my Tamil family, Sujith, Tyler, Parthi, Mario (Thambi), Anushani, Rudy, Ahilan, Meera, Kav, Tasha, Jellyfish, Nedra, and the many uncles and aunties who have offered me wisdom and Tamil food. The joy I have found in community with you has sustained my work in dark times. Whether gathered in Jaffna houses or New Jersey Turnpike motels, in the presence of your singular passion for this cause, I feel less alone.

To the women who have built walls of solidarity around me, indulged and informed radical thinking in so many ways, Asale, Aley, Rafia, Chandra, Ruchira, Angana, Jody, Ramatu, Jodie, Kimberlé: I am deeply grateful for your time, endless energy, and dedication to a conscious resistance. And to the next generation, born into politicized lives, Ana and the *Beyond Identity* fellows, you are my reminder that the fight, on multiple fronts, is critical for our collective survival.

———

The narratives in *Radicalizing Her* began to gather during my years at Operation USA, a uniquely empathetic collective that allowed me to both serve and reckon with the suffering of my people. Without the immense patience of Mark, Ed, and Jason at UCLA for my relentless insurgency I would not have a platform that can never be taken away. I will always be grateful to Zac for digging deeper into the roots of rebellion alongside me and raising our son to find the political potential in his boundless brilliance.

As my writing extracted itself from stilted academic prose, Kiese, Michael, and Katie would offer my words a soft entry into narrative nonfiction at *Guernica* magazine, which soon became both ally and home to my ambitious polemic desires. I am thankful to the thoughtful editors and brilliant writers of the continuing Female Fighter Series, who indulged an idea that quickly became a distinctive contribution to the literary landscape. John's endless generosity to emerging writers in general, and to my own essay "Captive," restored my faith in political writing. It was Michael and the other outliers of an often elitist literary world who inspired the creation of *Adi Magazine*, expertly guided by Meara Sharma, whose calm interventions have polished the precision of my own sentences and pushed the political imagination of the policy world.

My agent, Ria, first and foremost a comrade in the struggle, managed the angst of a first-time author while skillfully helping shape the final form these pages would take. Rakia was the first editor who saw this book for what it was, and Amy was the editor whose gentle approach allowed it to fulfill its destiny as an explicitly political project.

My now-scattered family does not just surround me; it constitutes me. My parents offered me opportunity, insisted on discipline, and never reneged on their promise to love unconditionally. My sister, my Akka, the first family writer (I did everything she did), teaches me every day why the fight to be happy is always worth it. My admiration for my brother, who absorbs adversity as a challenge to re-calibrate his life, has only grown stronger over the years. I grew through the extended love of my (one and only) Chithi, many aunties, and so very many cousins, piled on top of me in our own little village-in-exile. As my blended family settles into a new chapter, we have been so fortunate to have the immediate acceptance and love of Lyn, Bev, Chuck, and Teri.

To the female fighters, in Eelam and everywhere, you offered me intimate stories of pain, pride, and power, and I fear I had very little to give in return. This book was stalled for many years by my own scrutiny; an obsession to recreate an authentic representation of your courage, passion, complexity, and wisdom. It cannot be perfect, but I send this out into the world in hopes that the reader might feel the weight of your impact on the struggle. That your strength might change them forever, as it has me.

And to my (often hidden yet insistently present) Michael, whose intense editorial gaze has always insisted that my words find their intent and whose unshakeable love holds me together, every day.

NOTES

INTRODUCTION
1. Nayaki, interview by author, Killinochi, 2018.

CHAPTER 1: A BATTLEFIELD
1. Thamizhini, *In the Shadow of a Sword*, trans. Nedra Rodrigo (New Delhi: Sage Yoda, 2020).

2. Akila, interview by author, Washington, DC, 2017.

3. Internally Displaced Peoples (IDPs), interviews by author in various camps across the Vanni/Vavunya District, Sri Lanka, December 2009.

4. After having been the speaker of the Parliament in the 1960s, M. Sivasithamparam contested the general elections from the Nallur district with a Tamil nationalist party, the Tamil United Liberation Front, and won an overwhelming majority.

5. Thamizhini, *In the Shadow of a Sword*.

6. Sandra, interview by author, Bogotá, Colombia, 2016.

7. Meena Kandasamy, *Ms. Militancy* (Delhi: Peacock Books, 2011), 36.

8. Hannah Arendt, *On Violence* (New York: Harcourt, Brace & World, 1970), 35.

9. In "What Remains? The Language Remains," Arendt notes, "It just doesn't look good when a woman gives orders. She should try not to get into such a situation if she wants to remain feminine." In *Essays in Understanding, 1930–1954*, ed. Jerome Kohn (New York: Shocken Books, 1994), 2–3.

10. Rebecca Solnit, "Rebecca Solnit: A Rape a Minute, a Thousand Corpses a Year," *Guernica*, January 25, 2013, https://www.guernicamag.com/rebecca-solnit-a-rape-a-minute-a-thousand-corpses-a-year. Solnit argues that violence has a gender (male) and "is first of all authoritarian. It begins with this premise: I have the right to control you."

11. N. Sivanandan, "Ethnic Cleansing in Sri Lanka," speech delivered to "Marxism 2009" conference, Sri Lanka, 2009.

12. Janani, interview by author, Batticaloa, Sri Lanka, 2004.

13. Arlette Farge, *The Allure of the Archives* (New Haven, CT: Yale University Press, 2013), 11.

14. Kathirmathi Pathipaggam, *Heroes Day Addresses of V. Prabakaran* (Chennai: G. Elavazhagan, 2009).

15. Tamil Conference Notes, 1989.

16. Ted R. Gurr, *Why Men Rebel* (Princeton, NJ: Published for the Center of International Studies, Princeton University [by] Princeton University Press, 1970).

17. Karthika Nair, *Until the Lions: Echoes from the Mahabharata* (Brooklyn, NY: Archipelago Books, 2019), 197.

18. Simone de Beauvoir, *The Second Sex*, trans. H. M. Parshley (New York: Vintage Books, 1974), 162.

CHAPTER 2: THE STAGE

1. Sara, interview by author, Tunis, 2015.

2. Saba, interview by author, Tunis 2015.

3. Quintan Ana Wikswo, "Fieldwork," *Guernica*, March 2, 2015, https://www.guernicamag.com/fieldwork.

4. Miriam, interview by author, Tunis 2015.

5. Ofelia Medina, interview by author, Mexico City, 2014.

6. Dolores Dorantes and Jen Hofer, *Style = Estilo* (Chicago: Kenning Editions, 2016), no. 15.

7. Sergio González Rodríguez, *The Femicide Machine*, trans. Michael Parker-Stainback (Los Angeles: Semiotext(e), 2012), 37.

8. Yuri Herrera, "Diana, Hunter of Bus Drivers," *This American Life*, https://www.thisamericanlife.org/diana-hunter-of-bus-drivers.

9. Latha, interview by author, London, 2011.

10. Dorantes and Hofer, *Style = Estilo*, no. 17.

11. Kala, interview by author, Sri Lanka, 2011.

12. Fictionalized account drawn from actual testimony given to Nimmi Harasagama included in her forthcoming play, *A Homemade Kite*.

13. Testimony fictionalized for witness protection.

14. M. Neminathan, ed., *Tamil Eelam Literature* (London: Tamil Information Center, 1996), 108.

15. N. Malathy, *Tamil Female Civil Space: Its Evolution and Decline in Tamil Eelam* (Delhi: Aakar, 2019), 87.

16. Neminathan, *Tamil Eelam Literature*, 109.

17. Tiger cadres, interview by author, Batticaloa, Sri Lanka, 2005.

18. Neminathan, *Tamil Eelam Literature*, 109.

19. Tharani, quoted in Neminathan, *Tamil Eelam Literature*, 80.

20. Elder aunties remember the moment. Interview by author, Jaffna, Sri Lanka, 2018.

21. Activist interviews by author, Mexico City, translated by Ana-Puente Flores, 2014.

CHAPTER 3: THE STREETS

1. Tracy K. Smith, from "The Woman State," in *Adi Magazine*, Fall 2019.

2. De Beauvoir, *The Second Sex.*

3. An extended version of this argument was coauthored with Dr. Asale Angel-Ajani and appears in "Why Women Kill: On Gendered Violence and Our Inability to Understand Women's Rage," *Literary Hub*, April 10, 2020, https://lithub.com/why-women-kill.

4. Martha Craven Nussbaum, *Anger and Forgiveness: Resentment, Generosity, Justice* (New York: Oxford University Press, 2016).

5. Solnit, "A Rape a Minute."

6. Brittney Cooper, *Eloquent Rage: A Black Feminist Discovers Her Superpower* (New York: St. Martin's, 2018).

7. Soraya Chemaly, *Rage Becomes Her: The Power of Women's Anger* (New York: Simon & Schuster, 2019).

8. Arendt, *On Violence*, 63.

9. Rebecca Solnit, "Call Climate Change What It Is: Violence," *Guardian*, April 7, 2014, https://www.theguardian.com/commentisfree/2014/apr/07/climate-change-violence-occupy-earth.

10. Arendt, *On Violence*, 63.

11. Nair, *Until the Lions*, 32.

12. Mona Eltahawy, *The Seven Necessary Sins for Women and Girls* (Boston: Beacon Press, 2019), 108.

13. Jean-Paul Sartre, preface to Frantz Fanon, *The Wretched of the Earth* (1961), https://www.marxists.org/reference/archive/sartre/1961/preface.htm.

14. Mark Boyle, *Drinking Molotov Cocktails with Gandhi* (Hampshire, UK: Permanent Publications, 2015), 32.

15. bell hooks, "Moving Beyond Pain," Bell Hooks Institute, May 9, 2016, http://www.bellhooksinstitute.com/blog/2016/5/9/moving-beyond-pain.

16. Malathy, *Tamil Female Civil Space*, preface.

17. Marcelle Shehwaro, interviews by author, New York, 2016–19.

18. Arendt, *On Violence*, 63.

19. Facebook, https://zh-cn.facebook.com/Ms.Militancy/posts/it-is-impossible-for-tamil-people-to-forget-the-horrors-of-rape-committed-by-the/938609536161119.

20. Eltahawy, *The Seven Necessary Sins for Women and Girls*, 140.

21. In December 1991, Captain Vanathi's poems were published posthumously by the LTTE.

22. Thamizhini, *In The Shadow of a Sword.*

23. This argument is expanded in comparison with incarcerated women in the United States in Gowrinathan and Angel-Ajani, "Why Women Kill."

24. Thamizhini, *In The Shadow of a Sword.*

25. Akila, interview by author, Killinochi, 2019.

26. Thamizhini, *In The Shadow of a Sword.*

27. Mia Bloom, *Bombshell: Women and Terrorism* (Philadelphia: University of Pennsylvania Press, 2011).

28. James Baldwin, *Notes of a Native Son*, introduction by Edward P. Jones (1955; Boston: Beacon Press, 2012), 20.

29. Kimberlé Crenshaw, phone interview with author, March 2018. Parts of this interview appear in Nimmi Gowrinathan, "Kimberlé Crenshaw: Up in Arms, a Conversation About Women and Weapons," *Guernica*, March 28, 2018, https://www.guernicamag.com/kimberle-crenshaw-up-in-arms-a-conversation-about-women-and-weapons.

30. Email correspondence, December 2019.

31. Kiarra Sylvester, "Why Black Women Are Buying Guns," Your Tango, April 28, 2017, https://www.yourtango.com/2017302279/why-black-women-are-buying-guns.

32. Gowrinathan and Angel-Ajani, "Why Women Kill."

33. Racine, as told to Dr. Asale Angel-Ajani.

34. M.I.A., phone interview with author, 2019.

35. Dan Baum, "Happiness Is a Worn Gun," *Harper's Magazine*, August 2010, https://harpers.org/archive/2010/08/happiness-is-a-worn-gun/.

36. Neminathan, *Tamil Eelam Literature*, 79.

37. Adele Ann Balasingham, *Women Fighters of Liberation Tigers* (London: LTTE International Secretariat, 1993), 73.

38. Shailja Patel, *Migritude* (New York: Kaya Press, 2010), 7.

39. Vishaka, interview with author, 2019.

40. Thamizhini, *In The Shadow of a Sword.*

CHAPTER 4: A PANEL: THE THIRD LINE

1. Akila, personal interview, Sri Lanka, 2019.

2. Rodríguez, *The Femicide Machine*, 43.

3. Rodríguez, *The Femicide Machine*, 57.

4. Dr. Sonia Ahsan's comments at a conference co-organized with Dr. Dipali Mukhopadhyay, "Women Waging War," Columbia University, April 4, 2019.

5. Dorantes and Hofer, *Style = Estilo.*

6. Kate Cronin-Furman, Nimmi Gowrinathan, and Rafia Zakaria, "Emissaries of Empowerment," whitepaper published through the Colin Powell School for Civic and Global Leadership, City College of New York,

September 2017, http://www.deviarchy.com/wp/wp-content/uploads/2017
/09/EMISSARIES-OF-EMPOWERMENT-2017.pdf.

7. Assata Shakur, *Assata Shakur: An Autobiography* (Chicago: L. Hill, 1987).

8. Anne Carson, *Plainwater: Essays and Poetry* (New York: Vintage Books, 2000).

9. Email communication from white feminist scholar and policy analyst.

10. Marcelle Shehwaro, interviews by author, New York, 2016–19.

11. "The Future of Women and Violent Extremism," public panel, George Washington University, May 1, 2018.

12. "Linking Security of Women and Security of States: Policymaker Blueprint," Futures without Violence, May 2017, 11, https://www.futures withoutviolence.org/wp-content/uploads/FWV_blueprint_Final_web.pdf.

13. Email communication from white feminist scholar and policy analyst.

14. Email communication from senior official at the United Nations Development Program, 2015.

15. High-level donor at public event for UN Women.

16. Email communication from white feminist scholar and policy analyst.

17. Carson, *Plainwater*.

18. All references to "Speakers" come from the panel at George Washington University, "The Future of Women and Violent Extremism."

19. Thamizhini, *In The Shadow of a Sword*.

20. Thamizhini, *In The Shadow of a Sword*.

CHAPTER 5: THE SECOND LINE

1. Darshini, author's interview with refugees from Vanni, Sri Lanka, 2010.

2. Army officer, interview with author, Jaffna, 2014.

3. Father, personal interviews with Afghan refugees, Pakistan, 2012.

4. Artist rendering described to me by artist Vasuki Jeyasankar.

5. Thava, conversations inside Tamil Activist Workshop, Toronto, Canada, 2017.

6. Neminathan, *Tamil Eelam Literature*, 73.

7. Adele Balasingham, interview with author, London, 2018.

8. Vishaka, interview with author, 2019.

9. Malathy, *Tamil Female Civil Space*, preface.

10. Helen, interview with author, Asmara, Eritrea, 2006.

11. Thamizhini, *In The Shadow of a Sword*.

12. Father K, interview with author, Mannar, Sri Lanka, 2014.

13. Uzma Falak, "The smallest unit of time in Kashmir is a siege," *Adi*, Summer 2020, https://adimagazine.com/articles/the-smallest-unit-of-time.

14. Balasingham, *Women Fighters of Liberation Tigers*, 14.

15. Anuk Arupdpragasam, *The Story of a Brief Marriage* (New York: Flatiron Books, 2016), 35.

16. *The New Woman's Survival Catalog*, originally published 1973, ed. Rachel Valinsky and Rick Myers (Brooklyn, NY: Szaransky Printing Company, 2019), 73.

17. Maria, interview with author, Mexico City, 2014.

18. Roberto González Villarreal, *Ayotzinapa: La rabia y la esperanza* (Mexico: Editorial Terracotta, 2015), 140.

CHAPTER 6: THE FRONT LINES

1. Adele Balasingham, interview with author, London, 2018.

2. Malathi, interview with author, Eastern Sri Lanka, 2017.

3. D'lo, conversations with author, 2013–15.

4. Akila, interview with author, Sri Lanka, 2019.

5. Sandra, Whats App interview, 2020.

6. Chinua Achebe, *Girls at War and Other Stories* (London: Penguin, 2009), 111.

7. Meena Kandasamy, "The Orders Were to Rape You," *White Review* 28 (July 2020), https://www.thewhitereview.org/feature/meena-kandasamy.

CREDITS

Excerpt of Tracy K. Smith, "The Woman State," printed here with permission.

Excerpt from Vanathi's poem "Enathu peenaa" first appeared in *Vanathiyin Kavithaikal* (Tamil Eelam: LTTE Publication Division, 1992). The English translation is reprinted here with permission from Vanathi's estate and from the translator, Meena Kandasamy.

Excerpt from Meena Kandasamy's poem "Ms. Militancy" first appeared in her book *Ms. Militancy* (New Delhi: Navayana Press, 2010), 36. Reprinted here with permission.

Karthika Nair: Excerpts first appeared in Karthika Naïr, *Until the Lions: Echoes from the Mahabharata* (Brooklyn, NY: Archipelago Books, 2019), 32, 197. The first is from "Ulupi: The Capillaries of Cosmic Bodies." The second is from "Padati I. The Father/ Pawn Talk: Brass and String." Reprinted here with permission.

Excerpt from poem "No. 15" first appeared in *Style/Estilo* by Dolores Dorantes, trans. Jen Hofer (Chicago: Kenning Editions, 2016). Reprinted here with permission.

Excerpt from poem "No. 17" first appeared in *Style/Estilo* by Dolores Dorantes, trans. Jen Hofer (Chicago: Kenning Editions, 2016). Reprinted here with permission.

Excerpt from poem "No. 23" first appeared in *Style/Estilo* by Dolores Dorantes, trans. Jen Hofer (Chicago: Kenning Editions, 2016). Reprinted here with permission.

Excerpt of Uzma Falak's visual poem "The shortest unit of time in Kashmir is a siege" first appeared in *Adi Magazine* (July 2020). Reprinted here with permission.

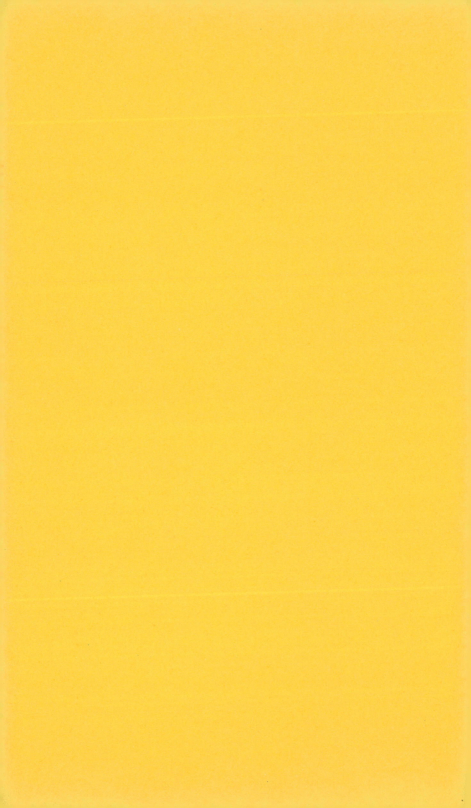